The Book of the

VESPA

A PRACTICAL GUIDE TO GENERAL MAINTENANCE AND RUNNING REPAIRS

BY

J. EMMOTT
M.I.F.Mech.

Published by

FLOYD CLYMER PUBLICATIONS

World's Largest Publisher of Books Relating to Automobile, Motorcycles, Motor Racing, and Americana

222 NO. VIRGIL AVENUE, LOS ANGELES 4, CALIFORNIA

Announcement

We have purchased the U.S. publishing rights for this fine book of the Vespa Motor Scooter from Sir Isaac Pitman and Sons, Ltd. of London.

The information in this book is authentic and will be of value to the Vespa owners and scooter enthusiasts.

We also have available a similar book on the Lambretta and books on other scooters will be forthcoming in the future.

Floyd Clymer

Publisher

CONTENTS

INTRODUCTION

Welcome to the world of digital publishing ~ the book you now hold in your hand, while unchanged from the original **1962** edition, was printed using the latest state of the art digital technology. The advent of print-on-demand has forever changed the publishing process, never has information been so accessible and it is our hope that this book serves your informational needs for years to come. If this is your first exposure to digital publishing, we hope that you are pleased with the results. Many more titles of interest to the classic automobile and motorcycle enthusiast, collector and restorer are available via our website at **www.VelocePress.com**. We hope that you find this title as interesting as we do.

NOTE FROM THE PUBLISHER

The information presented is true and complete to the best of our knowledge. All recommendations are made without any guarantees on the part of the author or the publisher, who also disclaim all liability incurred with the use of this information.

TRADEMARKS

We recognize that some words, model names and designations, for example, mentioned herein are the property of the trademark holder. We use them for identification purposes only. This is not an official publication.

INFORMATION ON THE USE OF THIS PUBLICATION

This manual is an invaluable resource for the classic **Vespa** enthusiast and a "must have" for owners interested in performing their own maintenance. However, in today's information age we are constantly subject to changes in common practice, new technology, availability of improved materials and increased awareness of chemical toxicity. As such, it is advised that the user consult with an experienced professional prior to undertaking any procedure described herein. While every care has been taken to ensure correctness of information, it is obviously not possible to guarantee complete freedom from errors or omissions or to accept liability arising from such errors or omissions. Therefore, any individual that uses the information contained within, or elects to perform or participate in do-it-yourself repairs or modifications acknowledges that there is a risk factor involved and that the publisher or its associates cannot be held responsible for personal injury or property damage resulting from the use of the information or the outcome of such procedures.

It is important that the reader recognizes that any instructions may refer to either the right-hand or left-hand sides of the vehicle or the components and that the directions are followed carefully. One final word of advice, this publication is intended to be used as a reference guide, and when in doubt the reader should consult with a qualified technician.

CHAPTER I

INTRODUCTORY

THE Douglas Vespa is a two-wheeled vehicle which completely breaks away from traditional motor-cycle design. It is propelled by a two-stroke engine of 125 c.c. capacity. Car-type seating gives weather protection and cleanliness for driver and passenger unequalled in the motor-cycling field. Planned for economy in use and maintenance, clean lines and streamlined contours have been used to maximum effect without detracting from ease of accessibility.

The power unit housing, of aluminium alloy, embodies the engine, clutch, gears, transmission and flywheel generator. Removal of the whole unit from the frame is simple and straightforward.

The flywheel generator is easily dismantled should the occasion arise. Beyond the simple maintenance procedure outlined on page 62, repair and replacement of any part of the flywheel generator should be entrusted to the makers: The B.T.-H. Co., Ltd., or their authorized service stations.

The frame of the Vespa is constructed of heavy-gauge steel pressings, electrically welded to a central longeron. An easily detachable tool and luggage compartment, in which is housed the battery carrier when fitted, is placed on the near side of the machine. A similar detachable cowling on the off side encloses the power unit.

All painted parts of the Vespa are stove-enamelled with polychromatic green paint.

In a compartment placed at the rear of the footplate is the sealed-off attachment for the carburettor.

The front wheel is held by a steering stem of cold drawn seamless steel tube, supported in bearings at the front of the main frame longeron. This stem has a cast-on bracket for the front mudguard and, at its lowest point, a tubular cross bearing is welded. This takes the spindle mounted on a trailing link, which incorporates a brake backplate. The hub of the quickly detachable wheel is mounted on a cross shaft joining the rear end of the link. Springing is by means of a long coil spring, inserted between another bracket on the steering stem and an anchorage on the radius arm.

The rear wheel is mounted on a light alloy rear suspension arm casting which pivots on a bearer-bolt, firmly held to the chassis. This casting embodies supports and brackets for engine unit, silencer, springing and damping assembly, and the rear brake mountings. Substantial rubber bushes are interposed between the suspension arm and bearer-bolt and require no maintenance.

1

This book is set out in chapters dealing with each of the various components. Where possible when dismantling, careful study of the appropriate illustration and laying out the thoroughly cleaned parts, in order of dismantling, will greatly assist speedy and accurate reassembly. Should the reader, however, still find difficulty in dismantling or assembly, it is strongly recommended that the Douglas Vespa agent be consulted. To persist in attempts to rectify an obscure trouble may result in serious damage.

In selecting agents, choice has fallen on those who have undertaken to provide adequate facilities for sales and service to all Douglas Vespa owners. The reader who is in any way uncertain, may thus expect to find—

1. A courteous welcome and enthusiastic assistance in all his problems.

2. At least one member of the staff with Douglas factory training.

3. A workshop equipped with the necessary tools to carry out a thorough overhaul of a Douglas Vespa.

4. A sufficient stock of genuine Douglas Vespa spare parts for all normal service and repair work. Here let it be added with all force, that none but genuine maker's spares should be used at all times.

By dealing only with a genuine Douglas Vespa agent, by taking pride both in the appearance of his machine and in his driving, the reader can be assured that the pride and pleasure he felt when first taking delivery will continue throughout the life of his machine.

CHAPTER II

MAINTENANCE AND CLEANING

To maintain the Douglas Vespa efficiently, a regular routine, diligently followed, is desirable. Great benefit can be derived by keeping a maintenance log.

On Taking Delivery. The following check is, in any case, worth while to gain familiarity with details of the design. If the machine is newly purchased from an authorized dealer, it will already have undergone a similar check. The new owner may, however, be taking delivery of a machine which has not had so much care or has travelled or been transported for some distance.

Carefully study the various fittings, grease nipples, nuts, bolts and screws, used on the Vespa. Check that all nuts and bolts are tight. Begin at the front of the machine and work to the rear, dealing with each side independently.

A correctly fitting spanner for every size of nut and bolt is essential for good maintenance. The Vespa has the advantage over many modern designs in that there is good room for spanner play at every point. Open-ended spanners have a habit of slipping, causing damage to paintwork, nut, bolt and fingers. Avoid them if possible.

Check the steering for loose bearings (*see* page 14) and check the tyre pressures (*see* page 11). See that brake adjustment, front and rear, is correct (*see* pages 15–16).

Maintain $\frac{1}{8}$ in. free play on the handlebar clutch lever before the actuating arm on the clutch case comes into operation.

Gear Case Lubrication. Keep the oil level up to the inspection hole in the gear case (*see* diagram of gear case). Over-filling may lead to a breakdown of the final drive oil seal, with leakage of gear case lubricant on to the brake linings, rendering the rear brake inoperative.

After 600 miles. At a period of 600 miles, the gear case should be drained. (The oil will run more easily when warm immediately after a run.) Refill with Castrol flushing oil, run the engine for a few minutes, to ensure thorough circulation and cleansing, and drain off. Afterwards, refill the gear case with new oil.

General Lubricating Hints. The writer recommends the use of the appropriate grades of oil of the following brands: Castrol, Shell, Mobiloil.

3

The writer has had particular satisfaction from the Wakefield Castrol range and his recommendations throughout this book are based accordingly. For consistency of performance, avoid changes in the brand of oil used. Oil with a viscosity higher than SAE 30 should on no account be used for engine or gear case.

After 1,000 miles. At a period of 1,000 miles rear brake operation is kept free by pulling the pedal out of the bush in the chassis (a spring clip on the pedal pin holds it in position). Wipe off the old lubricant and smear some Castrolease (heavy) grease on the pin, and inject a small quantity into the bush.

Apply a few drops of light cycle oil to the front brake and clutch handlebar lever fulcrum-pins and cable nipples. First, check that these nipples move freely in their holes in the levers. If tight, ease with a file. Approximately ninety-five per cent of cable breakages are caused by tight nipples.

To obtain silky working of these most frequently used controls, slip the cables from their levers and, holding them upright, work a little cycle oil between the casings and cable.

Both twist-grip drums should be greased, not oiled.

Apply a small amount of thin grease into the first and second ball joint of the gear-change mechanism. Lubricant of any description should be avoided on the final ball joint as accumulation of grit may cause sticking or rapid wear. Should the joint be stiff, pull out the split-pin and remove the rod in the manner described in engine removal (*see* page 27). Clean the ball and socket with petrol and reassemble with a small amount of graphite grease on the ball. This will last for a considerable period.

A good tip is to apply a few occasional drops of light oil to the key from the steering lock and to slide it in and out and to turn the lock a few times.

There are only two grease-gun nipples on the Vespa.

1. Speedometer gearbox.
2. Front hub trailing arm spindle.

Avoid over-greasing here, or failure of the grease retaining seals will result. Similarly, excessive use of the oil-can causes dust accumulations. Any such excess should therefore be wiped off with a clean cloth.

The above maintenance will ensure silky controls, which give carefree ease of driving, devoid of fear of annoying and avoidable road side hold-ups. Fifty per cent of involuntary stoppages can be traced to neglect.

At a Period not Exceeding 1,500 miles. The lubricating felt by the flywheel should be smeared with Castrolease (heavy) grease. Oil should not be used as it may find its way on to the points.

Every 5,000 miles. Remove the front links dust cover (*see* page 22) and lubricate with the grease-gun. Again, avoid over-greasing, for excess may contaminate the front brake linings.

Cleaning. Given normal usage, the Vespa should be cleaned and polished regularly (immediately prior to maintenance if this is due).

By far the easiest method of cleaning road machines is to use "Gunk" cleaner, obtainable at most agents. Apply with a rag to the body-work to avoid streaking, and with a brush to the wheels and gear case. Follow this by washing down with clean water and the whole machine will be gleaming without the need for hard work. When the paintwork has dried, a good wax polish will give a lasting shine. The polish can also be applied to all chromium plate.

Dry the H.T. plug lead and plug insulator should any water have inadvertently been splashed on these parts.

The use of paraffin as a cleaning material should be avoided. It invites rust and contaminates the tyres, besides making polishing a laborious task.

CHAPTER III

THE FUEL TANK

THE capacity of the main Vespa fuel tank is 1·1 gallons with an additional reserve of 0·2 gallons. A three-position fuel tap is operated by a "pull-push" rod, beneath the seat.

"Off"—Pushed right in.

"On (main)"—Pulled right out.

"Reserve"—Intermediate position with an indentation stamped on the rod, approximately ½ in. from the fully extended position.

Follow closely the instructions regarding the amount of oil per gallon of petrol shown on the filler cap. Avoid damage to the removable filter in the tank filler orifice. Avoid over-tightening the filler cap wing-nut. Damage to the sealing ring and the threads of the wing-nut and bolt will be the only result. The filler-cap sealing ring, the wing-nut and securing bolt can be renewed on withdrawing the respective split-pins. These split-pins, unlike every other split-pin on the Vespa, need not necessarily be renewed (unless broken) on reassembly.

The fuel tank is held in position by two steel plates, with cork washers, each plate secured by one bolt. The tightness of these bolts should be checked regularly. An anti-rattle cork washer is placed between the tank and the chassis and should the tank become loose it must be removed and all cork washers renewed, necessitating the following work.

To Remove the Fuel Tank. Unscrew and remove the nuts and plain washers securing the saddle springs to the chassis. Remove the nuts and locking washers securing the rear of the carrier to the chassis. Its nose being hinged, the saddle can now be swung forward. Remove the carrier.

Place the fuel tap in the off position. Disconnect the rubber fuel pipe from the carburettor by loosening its fixing clip to allow the hose to be pulled off its float chamber stub.

Unscrew the two securing bolts and remove the tank holding plates with cork washer; by easing the rear of the tank out first, it will easily come away from the chassis.

Should the holding plates have become strained from repeated tightening they can be restored to their original shape by placing one end in the vice and tapping the other gently. Avoid heavy blows which may damage the

6

paintwork. Should the anti-rattle cork washer persistently break down, a permanent cure will be effected if strips of old inner tube ¼ in. wide are cut and stuck in position by the use of "Bostick" adhesive on the underside of the lip of the fuel tank.

To Remove Fuel Tap Washers. Remove the tank as already described and drain. Pull out the split-pin securing the "pull-push" rod to the barrel

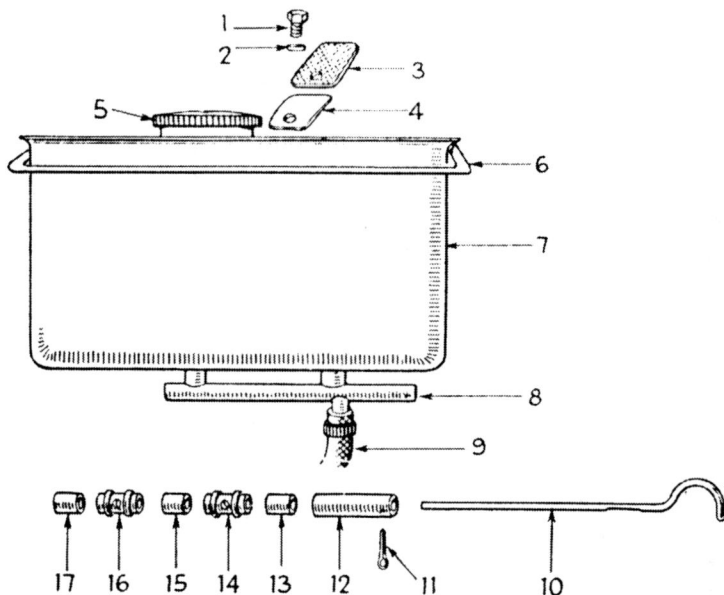

FIG. 1. FUEL TANK AND TAP

1. Tank securing bolt.
2. Plain washer.
3. Cork washer.
4. Tank securing plate.
5. Filler cap.
6. Anti-rattle cork washer.
7. Fuel tank.
8. Fuel tap main barrel.

9. Fuel hose to carburettor.
10. Pull-push rod.
11. Split-pin.
12. Brass guide bush for rod.
13. Rubber seal bush.
14. Brass distance-piece.
15. Rubber seal bush.
16. Brass distance-piece.

17. Rubber seal bush.

and pull the control rod clear. With a piece of bent wire remove from the barrel of the tap the two brass distance pieces together with the three rubber washers.

To Replace the Washers. Push into the barrel of the tap the washers and distance pieces in the order given on the next page.

1. Rubber washer, 2. Brass distance piece, 3. Rubber washer, 4. Brass distance piece, 5. Rubber washer.

Replace the control rod, securing with a new split-pin, size 1 in. $\times$ $\frac{1}{16}$ in. Should the tap be in any way hard to operate, remove as above and check that the control rod is not bent.

CHAPTER IV

WHEELS AND STEERING

THE wheels are of car-type, quickly detachable and interchangeable. After a few thousand miles, it is advisable to change them over, to obtain even tyre wear, as the rear wheel is called upon to do the most work.

The wheels consist of two metal pressings, bolted together by six studs, with nuts and lock washers. These are on the extreme circumference of the wheel flange and must not be mistaken for the securing nuts, which are four in number, with larger heads, and located in the centre of the hub flange.

Wheel Removal, Front. Place the machine on its stand, grasp the front tyre in the left hand, unscrew the four large nuts and place them, with their spring washers, on the footplate. The wheel can now be pulled off the hub studs.

Wheel Removal, Rear. Whilst still on its stand, the weight of the rear of the machine should be taken by a box, placed underneath the rear number plate or the kick-start pedal. The wheel can be locked by applying the rear brake while the hub nuts are undone.

Tyre Removal and Repairs. After removing the wheel—

1. Deflate the tube by removing the valve core, using the screwdriver end of the valve cap for this purpose.

2. Unscrew the six small nuts and place them, with their spring washers, on the footplate. The wheel can now be split and the cover and tube removed, care being taken that they remain together on the half of the rim with the valve hole, until the halves are completely separated.

With punctures it is advisable to have the part vulcanized. Your agent will attend to this for a few pence.

Tyre Replacement and Care. Before replacing, thoroughly dust the inside of the cover with french chalk. Ensure that the tube is dry and not twisted and insert it into the cover. Slightly inflate the tube, without the valve core, and allow it to become deflated again. Screw the valve core into position and again inflate slightly. Carefully place the valve through the hole in the rim and push the cover over the well of the wheel. After making sure that no part of the tube is showing, replace the second half. Replace the six spring washers and nuts, tightening each equally until all

9

are home. Inflate the tyre to its correct pressure and check the following before replacing the wheel—

1. The valve core must be screwed fully home, and air-tight. Test by inserting a drop of water in the valve. Make doubly sure by screwing on the valve cap. If the valve is leaking, fit a new core, obtainable from any

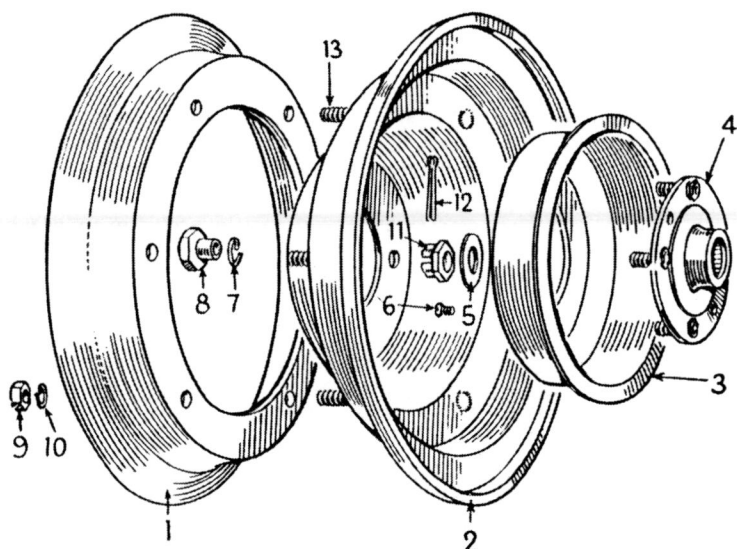

FIG. 2. REAR WHEEL

1. Wheel outer flange.	7. Wheel to hub spring washer.
2. Wheel inner flange.	8. Wheel to hub securing nut.
3. Brake drum.	9. Flange securing nut.
4. Rear hub.	10. Flange nut lock-washer.
5. Final drive washer.	11. Castellated nut for final drive shaft.
6. Brake drum securing screw.	12. Split-pin for castellated nut.

13. Flange studs welded to inner flange.

On the front wheel parts No. 5 and 11 are omitted. No. 4 is basically the same except that the oil seal spigot and splined shaft teeth are omitted and the front axle is substituted.

garage. (Valve Core: Schrader No. 4,000, Valve Caps: Schrader No. 880.)

2. With a blunt screwdriver, remove all small stones and flints from the tyre tread.

3. Remove any oil or grease from the cover with a clean rag, soaked in petrol. DO NOT dip the rag in your tank.

If, when on the road, you see a nail embedded in the tyre, do not pull it out unless you are prepared to mend a puncture there and then. Generally, a tyre will maintain pressure in such circumstances (unless the nail is wet) long enough to return to the workshop. The following summary of a test carried out by The Schrader Valve Co. confirms this point—

"A car was employed, on which the tyres had run 11,000 miles, representing one-third tread wear but actually in sound condition. Each tyre was inflated WHEN COOL to 28 lb per square inch. Valve caps were fitted to ensure double sealing of the valves. Five nails, each sufficiently long to penetrate the tube, were driven into each tyre, and the car driven off on a 1,000 mile journey, with instructions to keep the speed above average.

"During the first FIVE DAYS the test car covered 1,051 miles, representing 21,020 nail miles, without the tyres being re-inflated. As none had gone flat, this proved that the rubber tube clung to the nails making a partial seal."

Tyres maintained as above, and with pressures checked at regular intervals, have long life with freedom from puncture troubles.

TYRE PRESSURE CHART

(Tyre sizes 3·50 × 8)

Pressure (lb per sq. in.)

Rider of normal weight—	
Front tyre	12
Rear tyre	18
Rider and Pillion Passenger—	
Front tyre	14
Rear tyre	22
With Sidecar attached—	
Front tyre	18
Rear tyre	22
Sidecar tyre	18

Always check pressures when tyres are cool and never forget to replace valve cap after inflation or pressure check. Keep the inflator connexion free from dirt.

STEERING

The recommended period for the examination of the steering head balls and of the bearing surfaces, is between 6,000 and 10,000 miles. New ball bearings are always worth fitting at these examinations. Before commencing work, procure—

(a) 22 $\frac{1}{4}$ in. ball bearings.

(b) 35 $\frac{1}{8}$ in. ball bearings.

(c) Some Castrolease (heavy) grease.

(d) 2 pieces of stout wire bent to form a letter "S" similar to the ordinary butcher's hook.

To Dismantle the Steering Column. With the machine on the stand, remove the front wheel. Disconnect the speedometer drive cable by unscrewing the knurled nut on the underside of the instrument. Remove the split-pin from the first ball-joint of the gear-change rod at the handlebars. The adjusting screw of this joint can be slackened off sufficiently to allow the rod to be pulled gently off the ball, and rested on the footplate.

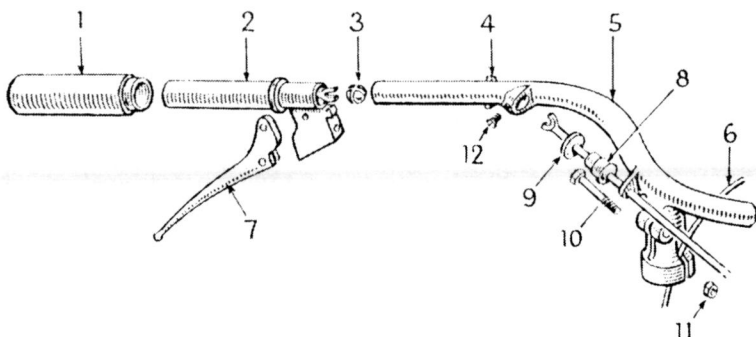

FIG. 3. HANDLEBAR GROUP

1. Twist-grip rubber.
2. Twist-grip gear-shift,
3. Ball joint.
4. Guide for twist-grip gear-shift.
5. Handlebar.
6. Front brake cable.
7. Clutch lever.
8. Gear-change rod guide bush.
9. Felt seal.
10. Handlebar lock bolt.
11. Nut for lock bolt.
12. Screw securing guide.

Remove the lever from the front brake handlebar control by unscrewing the pivot screw. Detach the cable.

Place the two "S" shaped wires, one on each side of the main longeron, on the inside edge of the front apron.

By completely removing the handlebar locking bolt, the handlebars can be lifted out and laid in the "S" hooks, thus preventing undue strain on the control or electric cables.

Place cloth or paper beneath the front of the machine to collect the balls which will drop when the steering assembly is dismantled. To avoid confusion on reassembly, they should be discarded.

Gently push the front brake cable through its guide hole and remove, in the following order—

1. Locking ring (use C spanner).
2. Tongued locking washer.
3. Top cone bearing (use pin spanner).

Gently lower the steering column to the ground, at the same time feeding the speedometer drive cable through the chassis.

Steering Head Races. Thoroughly clean and examine the top and bottom bearing cups and cones, for signs of pitting. The most minute pitting warrants renewal.

With a piece of $\frac{1}{2}$ in. rod, the old cups can be gently tapped out of the

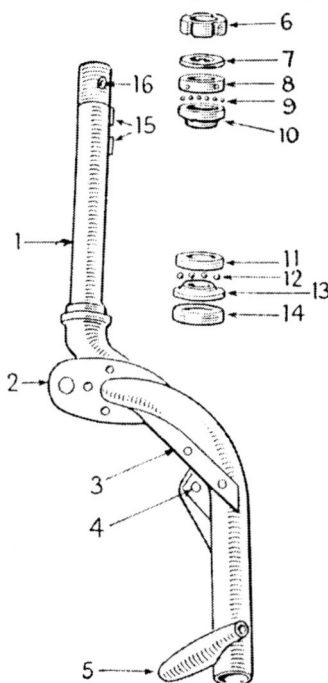

FIG. 4. STEERING COLUMN

1. Steering stem.	7. Locking washer.
2. Front mudguard bracket.	8. Top adjusting cone.
3. Front mudguard bracket (side securing).	9. Ball-roller bearings.
	10. Top bearing cup.
4. Top mounting for suspension spring.	11. Bottom bearing cup.
5. Mounting for trailing link spindle.	12. Bottom bearing ball-roller bearings.
6. Locking ring for adjustable cone.	13. Bottom bearing cone.
14. Dust-cover.	

The large hole in the mudguard bracket (No. 2) is for the speedometer driving cable.

steering body. Use care that they are driven out squarely and not tilted in their seatings. This could cause serious damage.

New cups can be tapped into their respective seatings with a hide-faced hammer, again keeping them square until finally home.

The bottom bearing cone, on the steering stem, can be gently removed with hammer and metal drift. Once again, use great care to avoid damage by tilting. If the dust cover beneath this bearing is in any way damaged a replacement is necessary.

To Reassemble the Steering Column. Place the dust cover on the stem and gently tap the new bottom cone into position. (Immersing the bearing in boiling water for a few moments greatly facilitates this work.)

Smear some Castrolease (heavy) grease on the bearing surface of the bottom cone and stick the 22 ¼ in. balls into position. In the same manner stick 35 ⅛ in. balls in the top cup.

Gently replace the steering column, through the two cups, taking care not to dislodge any balls held by the grease. The speedometer drive cable should be fed back through the chassis at the same time. The top cone bearing should be screwed down the stem and tightened until the bearings are closed up and there is no up and down movement of the steering stem although it will turn freely. Over-tightening causes stiff steering and rapid bearing failure.

Replace the tongued locking washer and screw on the locking ring until it is dead tight against the top cone. Test the steering again for free movement with no up and down play. If tightening the locking ring has made the movement less free, readjust as necessary. Pull the brake cable through its guide hole at the top of the stem. The handlebars can now be replaced. Before the handlebar locking bolt is finally tightened see that they are straight in relation to the wheel.

Push the speedometer drive inner cable on to the drive shaft of the instrument and replace the knurled nut (finger tight).

After greasing with Castrolease, the gear-change ball joint can be replaced in its socket and the adjusting screw screwed down tight and then slackened off half a turn, or to the nearest groove for the split-pin. (A new split-pin should always be used.)

Replace the wheel, and the front brake cable and lever. The job is now complete.

A few moments taking stock of the dismantling procedure is time well spent. When assembling begins, the parts can be replaced in exactly the same way as they were dismantled.

After a few hundred miles, test for any slackness in the steering stem. This should not occur if erection was perfect, but if it *has* happened, indicating settling down of the cups and cones, readjust accordingly.

CHAPTER V

BRAKES

The Vespa has excellent brakes on each wheel which, carefully used and maintained, will give long and faithful service. Sufficient adjustment is provided to cover every condition from new until the brakes need relining.

HINTS ON THE USE OF BRAKES

1. Use the engine and gears for all normal slowing down purposes.
2. Avoid excessive brake application, especially during icy or wet conditions.
3. Always apply the rear brake slightly more than the front.
4. Apply the brakes from time to time during wet weather. If water has found its way into the drums it can reduce efficiency temporarily. They will soon dry out from the heat of the applications.

Brake Adjustment, Front. An adjusting screw with a lock-nut is at the lower end of the brake cable. Proceed as follows—
1. Place the machine on its stand with the wheels in line fore and aft.
2. Apply the brake, once or twice to make sure that the actuating arm is working freely.
3. Spin the wheel in the direction of travel and listen for rubbing sounds. If the wheel is quite free, adjustment can be carried out. (Should rubbing occur, the wheel and brake drum should be removed for attention as described later in this chapter.)
4. Unscrew adjusting screw lock-nut.
5. Turn the brake adjusting screw until the brake begins to rub when the wheel is spun.
6. Turn back the adjusting screw two complete turns and tighten the lock-nut.
7. Test again for free running of the wheel. If adjustment has been correct, with the handlebar brake lever pulled until about ¾ in. separates the lever and the grip, the wheel should be locked.

Now inspect the brake cable as it protrudes from the bottom of the steering stem. It should be in a loop of approximately 2½ in. diameter, to allow easy working of the front springing. If the loop is smaller, gently pull on the cable and ease it out until the correct amount protrudes.

Spin the wheel and turn the bars gently from side to side. If the adjustment has been done correctly, the brake will remain off and will not stop the spinning during this test.

Brake Adjustment, Rear. The rear brake adjusting screw, on the underside of the rear suspension arm, is easily accessible at the rear of the off-side footplate.

With the machine on the stand and with a block under the rear number plate as previously described, proceed as follows—

1. Make sure that the gear lever is in neutral.
2. Apply the brake pedal to ascertain free working without sticking.

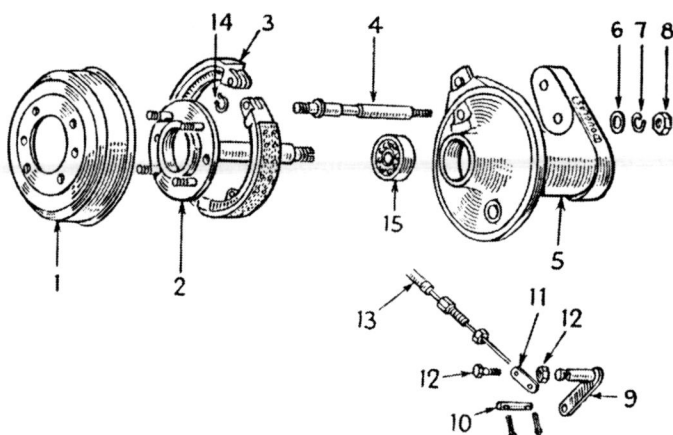

FIG. 5. FRONT BRAKE

1 Brake drum.	8. Pivot bolt securing nut
2. Front hub and axle.	9. Actuating lever.
3. Brake shoes.	10. Cable anchor pin.
4. Brake shoe pivot bolt.	11. Anchor plate.
5. Oscillating hub.	12. Cable pinch-bolt and nut.
6. Plain washer.	13. Front brake cable.
7. Spring washer.	14. Brake shoe securing circlip
	15. Axle bearing.

Adjustment is carried out in the same way as for the front brake, allowing ¾ in. between brake pedal and footplate when the wheel is locked.

Test brake adjustments regularly to ensure safety at all times. Do not wait till an emergency before realizing that the brakes are the most important part of any mechanically propelled vehicle.

Re-lining. If, having already used all the adjustment, the brakes no longer have their usual stopping power, the brake shoes require re-lining. This is a straightforward matter if the following parts and tools are first obtained:

1. Brake lining material especially made for the Vespa. (Your agent stocks the correct Ferodo linings with rivets.)
2. A rivet anvil, obtainable from most garages or all Ferodo agents.

3. A light, flat pane hammer and also a small, sharp, cold chisel. As front and rear brakes are of identical construction, the following procedure applies to either—

Remove the wheel. The brake drum will be seen to have two counter-sunk screws between the wheel studs. Unscrew these and pull the drum off the hub and brake assembly.

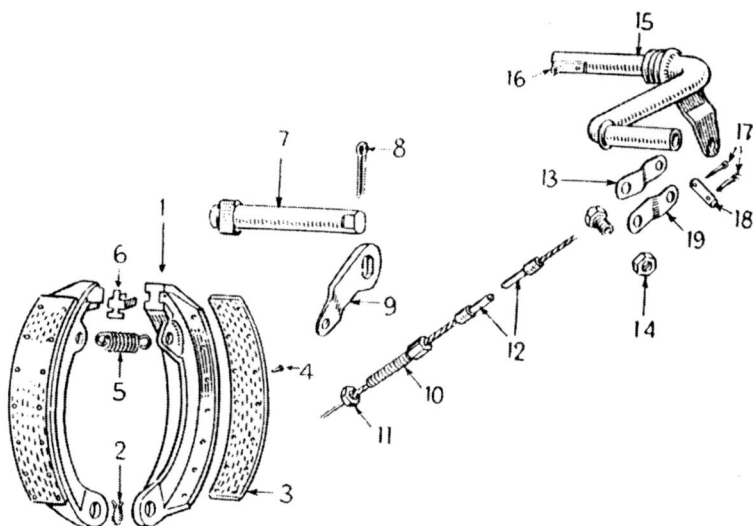

FIG. 6. REAR BRAKE

1. Brake shoe.	10. Operating cable adjusting screw.
2. Circlip.	11. Adjusting screw lock-nut.
3. Brake lining material.	12. Operating cable (outer and inner).
4. Brake lining rivet.	13. Cable pinch-bolt.
5. Shoe return spring.	14. Pinch-bolt nut.
6. Shoe fulcrum pad.	15. Rear brake pedal.
7. Brake operating shaft.	16. Pedal securing spring.
8. Split-pin for operating shaft.	17. Split-pins for anchor pin.
9. Actuating plate.	18. Anchor pin.
19. Anchor plates.	

The front brake is the same except that parts No. 15, 16 and 17 are omitted and parts No. 7 and 9 are welded to each other.

Slacken off all the adjustment of the brake adjusting screw. The brake shoes pivot on one boss, where they are held in position by a circlip, whilst at the opposite end the cam operated by the brake control expands the shoes against the drum.

Gently ease the circlip out of its groove on the pivot boss, taking care to avoid loss when suddenly released.

To ensure reassembly in the correct order, place a small mark on one shoe and the adjacent part of the brake backplate.

The shoes can be pulled off their pivot boss and the brake return spring removed.

Fitting Linings. Clamp the shoe in the vice with its underside uppermost and chisel off the rivet ends. With a screwdriver the old lining can now be pulled away.

Thoroughly clean all the brake parts and drum with either clean petrol or "Gunk" (*see* page 5). The shoes and the hands must be dry and clean before the lining material is handled.

By clamping the new lining material to the shoe in the same position as the old, using the vice, the holes for the rivets can be drilled, using the holes in the shoe as a guide.

To countersink the holes for the rivet heads, a round piece of wood, drilled down its centre and slipped over the drill, of sufficient length to allow the end of the drill to enter the lining material two-thirds of its thickness is ideal.

After inserting the rivet through the lining and the shoe, it should be cut off leaving approximately ⅛ in. protruding from the underside for riveting.

Tightly clamp the rivet anvil in the vice. By holding the lining square with the shoe and with its head laid on the anvil, the rivet can be fastened with a few light blows. Over-tightening of the rivets only leads to splitting the material and possibly the shoe.

Using a clean coarse file, the lining can be gently eased down level, with the sides of the shoe and the ends gently sloped. With the ends so tapered, optimum braking is achieved without harshness and chattering.

The return spring should be replaced in its original position. The shoes are now ready for fitting and should be kept clean and dry until required.

The Operating Mechanism. A small amount of wear on the flats of the cam or pivot boss can be dealt with by a competent welder for a few pence. The only remedy for excessive wear (caused by lack of grease) is renewal of the parts.

After applying a small amount of Castrolease to the pivot bearing and actuating flats, the brake shoes can be returned to their correct position. Take care that no grease gets on to the linings.

When replacing the spring circlip, make sure that it beds correctly into the groove in the pivot boss.

The Brake Drum. Attention should now be turned to the brake drum. If there is any scoring of the braking area (generally caused by rivet heads insufficiently countersunk), it can most likely be turned out by your local agent. Heavy scoring, of course, necessitates a new drum. Failure to examine the drum and correct such faults will lead to rapid wear of the new linings.

After replacing the brake drum and its countersunk screws, the wheel can be fitted and the brake adjusted. The linings will bed down after approximately 100 miles so it is advisable, once again, to remove the brake drum when this figure has been reached and gently ease down any high spots on the linings with a clean file (high spots are revealed on the material by shiny black areas) until a uniform matt surface appears.

Oil Leaking to Rear Brake. Oil from the gear case may find its way on to the rear brake shoes and drum, rendering the brake inoperative. This can be due to two causes:

1. Most frequently, due to precipitate action after having failed to keep a routine check of the oil level in the gear case. Realization is often followed by indiscriminate filling of the case above the level.

2. Breakdown of the final drive oil seal.

To Rectify Over-filling. Drain the case to the correct level. Remove the split-pin from the main axle nut in centre of wheel, unscrew the nut and remove the plain washer. The wheel, brake drum and its splined flange may be withdrawn as one unit from the rear suspension arm casting and the splined final drive shaft.

Thoroughly wash all traces of oil off the brake parts, which still remain in position on the rear suspension arm. If the material has become saturated with oil, new linings are essential.

To Replace the Final Drive Oil Seal. Having removed the wheel and hub unit, the oil seal can be seen surrounding the splined final drive shaft. The seal can be removed by inserting a stout screwdriver inside the seal and gently easing round the whole edge. Care must be taken to avoid damage to the seal housing.

The new oil seal is inserted, open spring loaded side first, taking care to ensure a square entry and bringing right home without damage either to seal or housing.

The brake and rear wheel unit can then be reassembled and the plain washer and castellated nut of the final drive shaft replaced. If the split-pin hole in the shaft fails to correspond with a slot when the nut has been thoroughly tightened, a thinner plain washer must be used. ON NO ACCOUNT MUST THE NUT BE LOOSENED to allow easy entry of the split pin. Neither must it be over-tightened for the same purpose.

A new split-pin ($\frac{1}{8}$ in. × $1\frac{1}{2}$ in.) must be fitted whenever the hub has been removed.

CHAPTER VI

THE STEERING LOCK

THE barrel-type lock on the main longeron operates by moving a plate against a stop, brazed to the steering stem, locking the steering at full left lock.

The two main causes of damage resulting in the inability of the lock to function are—

1. Wrenching the handlebars when the lock is in the closed position.

2. More frequently, due to riding the machine when the lock is minus the key.

Examination of Lock. Remove the steering stem and front wheel assembly (*see* page 9). Examine the stop plate for failure of the brazing.

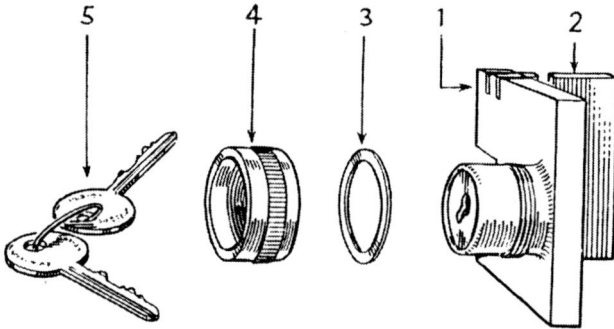

FIG. 7. STEERING LOCK

1. Steering lock main body.　　　3. Plain washer.
2. Hinged locking plate.　　　4. Locking ring.
5. Yale-type keys.

Operate the lock by turning the key at the same time looking down at the lock plates inside the steering body.

Broken Stop. Should the stop plate be broken away from the steering stem, it can be re-brazed. Care must be taken to clean away surplus brass after brazing, or the key cannot be withdrawn from the lock after turning.

Removing the Lock. To remove the lock from the chassis, the bottom bearing cup must be removed from the steering body to allow the lock to drop through the bearing housing. Remove the key from the lock and unscrew the locking ring round the key barrel. By careful feeding downward, past the lighting cables inside the steering body, the lock can now be withdrawn. The lock complete with two keys should then be handed to the Vespa agent for repair or replacement.

Replacing the Lock. By hooking a piece of thin copper wire round the repaired or new lock, it can be pulled up the steering body (avoiding the lighting cables once again) and refastened (finger-tight) in its location hole in the chassis. Replace the steering assembly and handlebars (*see* page 14). Turn the handlebars as far to the left as they will go and turn the key in the lock. By gently turning the handlebars back until they come up against the lock stop, the lock can be placed square in relation to the stop on the steering stem. Holding the lock in this position, finally screw the barrel locking ring dead tight.

Finally, place the key in the lock with a few drops of oil and turn once or twice to lubricate the wards.

CHAPTER VII

FRONT SUSPENSION

THREE good rules for efficient maintenance of the front suspension unit are—
1. Remove the front wheel.
2. Ensure cleanliness at all times.
3. Examine the assembly of the unit thoroughly before commencing dismantling. During dismantling, lay all parts on a clean surface in order of removal, to ensure correct reassembly.

Front Wheel Axle Assembly. Remove the brake drum, and dismantle the brake shoes to avoid possible contamination of the lining material (*see* page 17).

Remove the link dust-cover, complete with speedometer gearbox and drive cable, by unscrewing the fixing bolt on the face of the cover. This bolt has a distance piece inside the cover.

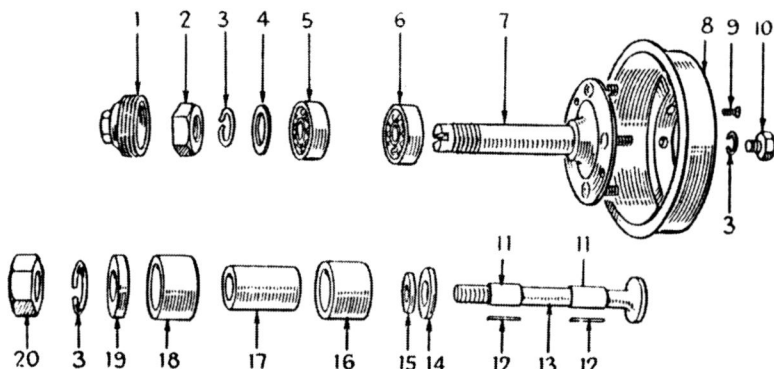

FIG. 8. FRONT SUSPENSION: AXLE ASSEMBLY

1. Grease cap.	11. Ground diameter for roller track.
2. Axle locking nut.	12. Needle roller.
3. Spring washer.	13. Trailing link spindle.
4. Plain washer.	14. Grease seal.
5. Axle bearing.	15. Roller retaining washer.
6. Axle bearing.	16. Liner for rollers.
7. Axle and front hub.	17. Liner distance-piece.
8. Front brake drum.	18. Liner for rollers.
9. Drum securing screws.	19. Grease seal.
10. Wheel securing nut.	20. Spindle locking nut.

22

Undo the grease cap for the front wheel axle and, after unscrewing the axle locking nut with spring and plain washers, the axle can be tapped through the two roller bearings in the revolving hub and out of the two trailing links. Use a BRASS punch and a light hammer. Heavy blows can damage the speedometer drive slot in the end of the axle. The revolving hub can now be removed from the arms. Should new axle bearings be

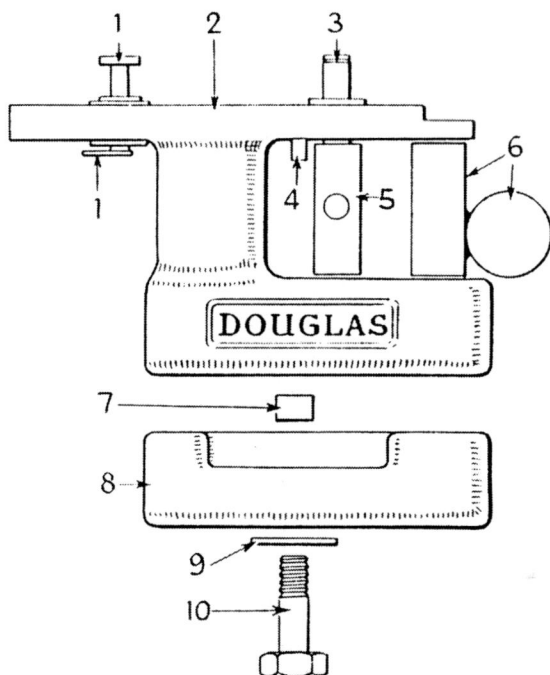

FIG. 9. FRONT SUSPENSION: OSCILLATING HUB

1. Brake actuating assembly.	6. Mounting for trailing link spindle.
2. Hub casting.	7. Distance-piece for cover.
3. Brake shoe pivot.	8. Dust cover.
4. Cable adjusting screw bracket.	9. Plain washer.
5. Bottom spring trunion.	10. Dust cover securing bolt.

required, the old ones can be knocked out of the hub with a punch passed through the hub shell from the opposite side. After new bearings have been pressed into position, the axle can be replaced and firmly tightened, holding hub and trailing links as one oscillating assembly. Make sure that the plain washer, spring washer and axle nut (shouldered side first) are replaced in that order.

Repack the grease cup with Castrolease and screw it into position. Replace the dust cover (not forgetting the fixing bolt distance piece) and, before attempting to tighten the bolt, turn the hub until the speedometer drive engages.

To Remove the Front Spring. Remove the front wheel, brake drum, and

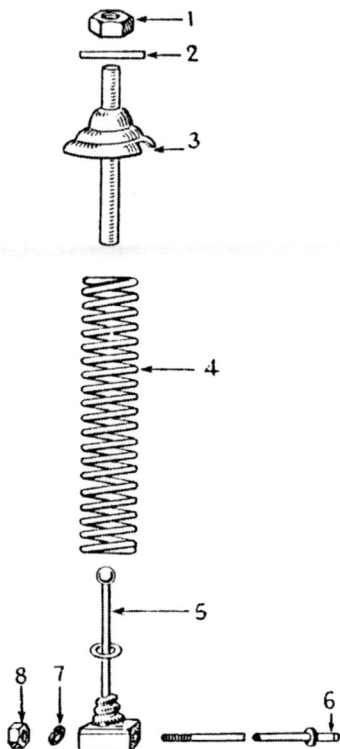

FIG. 10. FRONT SUSPENSION: FRONT SPRING

1. Top anchor nut.	5. Bottom spring trunion and guide rod.
2. Plain washer.	6. Trunnion bolt.
3. Top spring trunion and guide bush.	7. Spring washer.
4. Suspension spring.	8. Trunnion bolt securing nut.

hub dust-cover. Unscrew the anchor nut fixing the top of the spring to the bracket on the steering stem.

Inside the dust cover is a central nut, with spring washer, holding the bottom spring trunnion assembly. Remove this nut and tap the trunnion bolt back through the off-side trailing link sufficiently to allow removal of the spring.

If the guide rod is broken, a complete new trunnion is required. To fit, grip the spring in a vice and, with a rod through the trunnion hole, unscrew the old trunnion body and screw the replacement into the coils of the spring.

The trunnion guide rod and bush should not be lubricated, otherwise road filth attracted will cause rapid wear.

To Remove the Trailing Link Spindle from the Steering Stem. Remove the front wheel, brake drum, brake assembly and front spring as already described.

Unscrew the locking nut of the trailing link spindle and remove the spring washer, place a clean newspaper beneath the front suspension

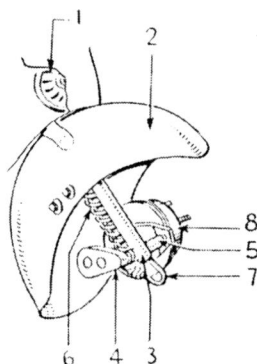

FIG. 11. FRONT SUSPENSION: STEERING STEM

1. Horn.	5. Mounting for trailing link spindle.
2. Front mudguard.	6. Suspension spring.
3. Steering stem.	7. Front brake cable.
4. Dust cover.	8. Brake drum.

assembly and tap the spindle out of its bearings. These consist of two sets of 18 needle rollers running in two liners a press fit in the bracket welded to the steering stem. The liners are separated by a distance piece. If in need of replacement, the liners and washers should be carefully tapped out with a punch. Avoid excessive force and take care not to damage the bore of the bracket. Clean the bore and pull the new liners into position with a long bolt and washers.

Reassemble Link Spindle. Replace in this order—grease seal, liner, distance piece, liner, grease seal and rollers (held in position with Castrolease), roller retaining washer and grease seal.

Hold the hub and link casting in position and thread the spindle (from the offside, threaded end first) through the hole in the link and through the bearing.

Fit the spring washer and tighten the locking nut. Test the trailing links for free travel, replace the front spring, brake assembly, front wheel and, finally, the dust cover (not forgetting the distance piece for the dust cover bolt).

Push the machine off the stand, and, if correctly assembled, the front springing will work smoothly when weight is applied to the handlebars with the front brake on.

CHAPTER VIII

REAR SUSPENSION

The rear wheel of the Vespa has soft springing comparable with that of a modern car. A light alloy casting forms a combined radius suspension arm and engine bearer. This is controlled by a large section three-rate coil spring with a hydraulic damper unit.

Three rubber buffers on the suspension arm prevent bottoming of the spring and damper unit.

The oil-controlled damper should be inspected once every 1,000 miles to see if it needs topping up. It should be kept clean externally and free from rust. By keeping to one brand of oil, the unit will give constant performance over very long periods.

As the engine unit is bolted to the main suspension arm, it must be removed before the rear suspension can be dismantled.

To Remove Engine Unit. Place a block underneath the rear number plate. Remove the rear wheel, complete with rear brake drum and splined flange, from the final drive shaft (*see* page 9). This will reveal the clutch cable on the near side engine case. Disconnect the cable from the actuating arm.

Remove the split-pin from the gear-change-rod ball and socket joint on the offside of the engine gear case. Unscrew the adjusting screw a few turns to allow the rod to be lifted off the ball joint.

Remove the H.T. lead completely. Unscrew the small screws on the low tension pick-up plug and remove the lighting cables (*see* page 64). Remove the silencer complete, by unscrewing the pinch-bolt and securing bolt (*see* page 38).

Disconnect the induction pipe from the cylinder barrel (three nuts and locking washers).

Unscrew the two bolts holding the lower spring and damper anchorage plate to the rearmost end of the suspension arm. There is a third bolt, nearer to the brake plate, which is not used to hold the anchorage plate. It should be completely removed.

Loosen the cylinder base steady-bolt connecting the crankcase mouth to the suspension arm. By lifting the cylinder barrel, the engine unit can now be pulled out of its bearer, care being taken not to damage the gear-change rod in the process. (*See* pages 40, 32, 61 for further work on engine, carburettor and ignition system.)

1. Suspension arm.
2. Rear brake plate.
3. Brake shoe anchor.
4. Silencer bolt bracket.
5. Suspension arm bearer-bolt.
6. Securing bolt.
7. Spring washer

8. Rubber buffer.
9. Rubber buffer.
10. Engine steady clamp bracket.
11. Engine unit clamp bolt.
12. Spring washer.
13. Plain washer.
14. Securing nut.

15. Spring anchor bolt.
16. Damper securing bolt.
17. Bottom damper bracket.
18. Plain washer.
19. Spring washer.
20. Silencer securing bolt.
21. Bottom damper fixing bush.

22. Rubber buffer.
23. Plain washer.
24. Rear damper.
25. Rear suspension spring.
26. Top spring trunnion.
27. Rubber buffer.
28. Top damper fixing stud.

29. Carrier securing nut.
30. Leather washer.
31. Rubber pad.
32. Top alloy fixing bracket.
33. Plain washer.
34. Spring washer.
35. Top bracket securing bolt.

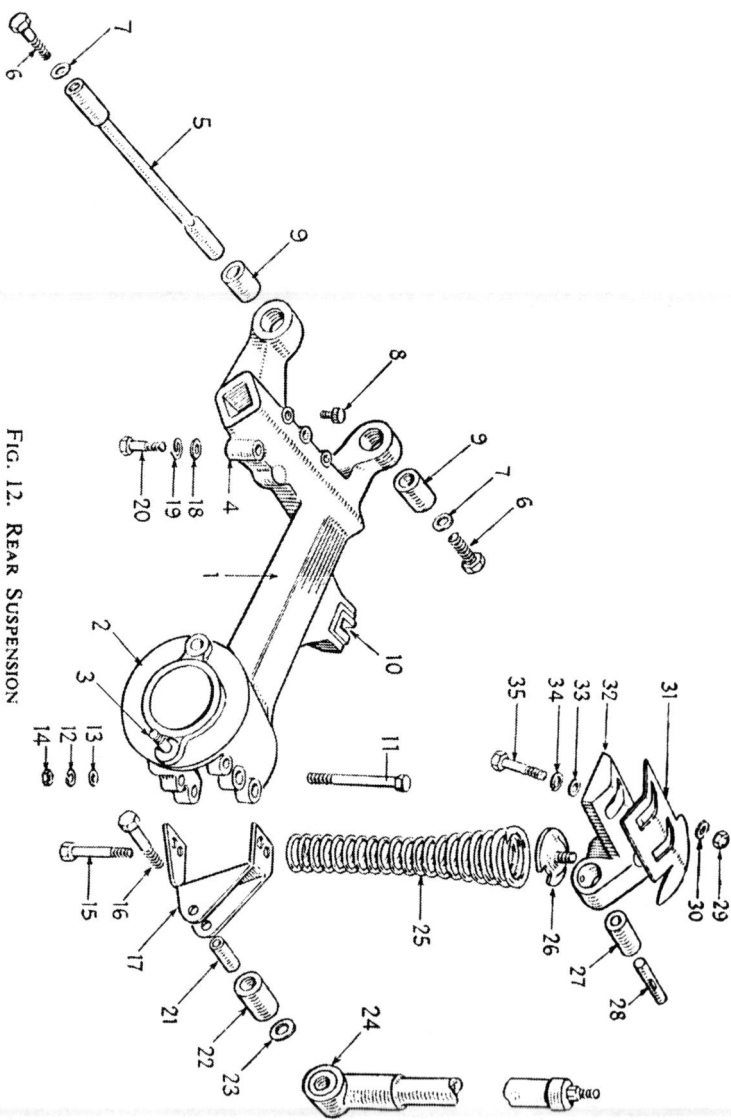

FIG. 12. REAR SUSPENSION

To Dismantle the Rear Spring Assembly. Remove the luggage carrier (*see* page 6) and the two leather washers between the carrier and the chassis. This will reveal two studs which hold the top damper and spring anchorage plate to the chassis. Push the bolts downwards and remove them. (There is a rubber pad placed between the top anchorage plate and the chassis. Put this in a safe place in readiness for reassembling.) Now remove the two bolts, already loosened, of the lower anchorage and the spring and damper assembly can be lifted clear. Place a clean sack under the suspension arm and lower it to the floor.

To Remove Rear Suspension Arm. Further to the above work, unscrew the rear brake and clutch cable adjusters and remove the control cables from their respective slots.

Unscrew the nut and lift clear the bolt holding the gear-change-rod clip to the foot plate. By unscrewing the two bearer-rod bolts, one on each side of the main longeron, the suspension arm can be pulled clear of the chassis. The suspension arm spindle can now be tapped out of the rubber bushes (using a brass punch).

To Renew the Suspension Arm Rubber Bushings. Press the rubber bushes out of their seatings. The replacement bushes should be dipped in clean petrol immediately prior to insertion.

By further dipping the suspension arm spindle into clean paraffin, the remounting of the newly bushed suspension arm on to the longeron will be easily accomplished.

To Renew the Rubber Buffers. The three rubber buffers can be replaced without removing the suspension arm. By allowing the arm to rest on the floor, twist the old buffers out of their seatings in the cross arm behind the hinges. Replacements should have their smaller diameters dipped in petrol before insertion.

By dipping rubber bushes or buffers in petrol, a semi-bonding action takes place immediately the petrol has evaporated. Fitting must, therefore, be speedy and completely home. ON NO ACCOUNT MUST ANY OIL OR GREASE BE USED WITH RUBBER COMPONENTS.

The rubber inserts in the damper-unit anchorages are specially bonded in manufacture. Should they fail, the anchorages must be returned to the agent for renewal.

When reassembling the rear suspension, smear the thread of all bolts and nuts with graphited grease to ensure easy dismantling on any future occasion.

Replacement of the rear suspension is in exactly the reverse order, but do not forget to feed the gear-change-rod through the engine-unit channel when the unit is being positioned in the suspension arm. DO NOT forget the rubber pad between the top anchorage plate and the chassis.

The top end of the rear suspension spring (the bigger diameter) is positioned in a well in the top anchorage plate by a locating bolt. Take care that it remains completely central during assembling. The bottom end of the spring is held in position by the outer engine securing bolt.

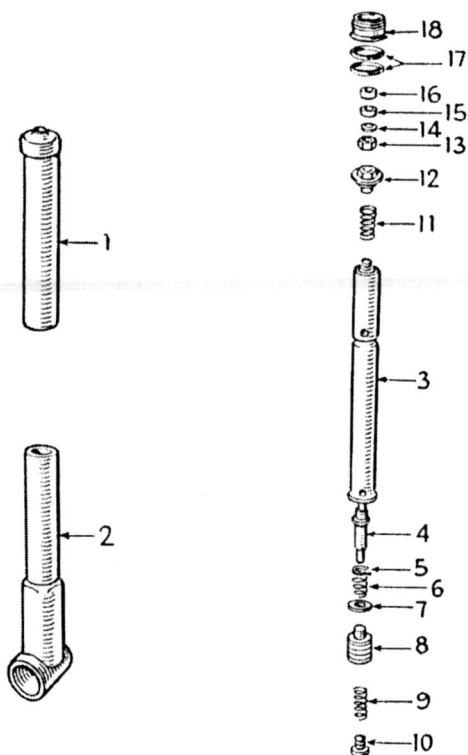

FIG. 13. REAR DAMPER

1. Top outer cover.	10. Spring securing nut.
2. Bottom oil container.	11. Top overload spring.
3. Damper main tube.	12. Main tube guide bush.
4. Operating rod.	13. Overload spring nut.
5. Circlip for control release valve.	14. Rubber buffer.
6. Release valve spring.	15. Plain steel washer.
7. Control plate.	16. Oil seal ring (for operating rod).
8. Piston type valve.	17. Oil seal rings (for bottom oil container).
9. Bottom overload spring.	

18. Knurled locking ring.

N.B. The whole assembly is secured in the bottom oil container and the top of the operating rod is secured in the top damper fixing stud (*see* illustration on rear suspension).

The Rear Damper Unit. To dismantle, the rear spring and damper unit must be completely removed from the rear suspension arm and chassis as

already described. With the hydraulic damper removed from the anchorage plates and cleaned, proceed as follows—
1. Unscrew the dust cover locking nut at the top of the unit.
2. Lift off the tubular dust cover.
3. Unscrew the knurled top sealing bush, now revealed.
4. Lift the complete oil control assembly upwards.

If without defects, the unit should be washed clean in petrol and filled with new Castrol Shockol. Should the damper not be functioning correctly, this can, broadly, be ascribed to either of the following—
1. Oil too old.
2. Control valve not functioning.

For the first, *complete* replacement of the oil is all that is needed.

For the second, service replacements are obtainable at your dealer's, but if the occasion warrants dismantling, proceed in the following order—

To Dismantle and Reseat the Oil Control Valve. Remove the valve spring nut, valve spring, oil valve plate and damper body. Using fine carborundum paste, lightly grind the two faces together, thoroughly clean off all traces of grinding paste and reassemble as dismantled.

Refill the reservoir with *new* Castrol Shockol and replace the dust cover.

ON NO ACCOUNT must lubricant be used between the dust cover and the main body of the damper.

CHAPTER IX

THE CARBURETTOR

The "Amal" carburettor used has been specially designed for the Vespa, with minimum risk of annoying delays due to the use of small jets.

How it Works. The throttle controls the mixture automatically according to the engine speed. The full power control of the mixture is by a submerged main jet, feeding the engine through a needle jet varied by a taper needle. This taper controls the effective jet orifice to allow a small flow of petrol at lesser throttle openings, increasing in volume up to the fully open position, when the flow is governed by the submerged jet, providing a means for enriching or weakening the mixture relative to the throttle movement. The needle is located in the throttle by a spring clip. A series of grooves, in the needle, any of which can be engaged in the clip, permit the needle to be raised or lowered relative to the throttle.

For idling, at the almost closed throttle position, the parallel portion of the needle enters the bore of the needle jet. The differences in diameter are so small that it is not impossible for gumming up to take place, due to the petrol and oil system, after the machine has been left overnight. This can be instantly cleared by opening the throttle. The throttle slide is cut away at its bottom on the side away from the engine. Throttles with various degrees of cut-away are available, the steeper giving weaker and the more shallow giving richer mixture strength at idling and slow running.

The petrol feeds into the top of the float chamber in which a constant level is maintained. Petrol flows to the main jet through a drilled passageway.

GENERAL MAINTENANCE

Keep the float chamber and its top fuel orifice free from impurities (the commonest cause of flooding). Otherwise if flooding occurs, remove the carburettor by the following method—

Detach the air cleaner by removing two wing-nuts with locking washers. Gently pull the air cleaner off its fixing studs and unhook the choke control wire. Remove the throttle control cable from the hinged control arm and its fixed abutments. Remove the rubber hose from the fuel supply pipe on the float chamber cap and, by slackening off the collar tightening screw, the carburettor can be pulled off the induction pipe. Unscrew the central plug securing the banjo end of the fuel supply pipe to the float chamber cap, taking care to avoid damaging the gauze filter located in the banjo. Remove the two lid securing screws and lift the float chamber lid.

The Float Chamber. Check the float and float needle units. The needle must not be bent nor the float punctured (test by shaking). The tickler in the float chamber lid must work freely and spring back. If the taper seating of the needle is deeply grooved, a new needle and float will be necessary. Thoroughly clean the float chamber, particularly the bottom needle guide and that in the lid.

Replace the float assembly (blunt end of needle first) and, before positioning the float chamber lid, ensure that the bottom of the float needle is in its guide hole on the floor of the chamber. Tighten the lid screws.

The Throttle Slide. Should the throttle become slack through long usage, it must be replaced to maintain the engine's slow running capabilities. At such long periods the needle jet should also be replaced. This will have worn slightly through the movement of the needle, causing a richer mixture than is controllable within the range of needle adjustment. A new needle jet deserves a new needle, an inexpensive item which will recover its cost many times in saving of fuel.

The Air Cleaner. At least once every 6,000 miles the air cleaner should be removed and washed in clean petrol. When dry it should be thoroughly soaked in engine oil, hung up for about ten minutes to allow excess oil to drain off and replaced.

The Induction Pipe. Should the carburettor be removed, plug the end of the induction pipe with clean cloth to prevent foreign matter getting into the engine.

When refitting, make sure the carburettor is right home before locking the collar tightening screw. Never fit a carburettor on to the steel induction pipe unless it is a good close fit (although not so tight as to require force). A little oil on the pipe simplifies fitting. If slackness has occurred, a new mixing chamber is the only cure.

Tuning the Carburettor. When describing this work, the mixture referred to is the proportion of petrol and air to secure optimum performance. Do not confuse this with the mixture of oil with petrol.

To tune-up precisely throughout the throttle range, consider four throttle positions—
1. Throttle slightly open as for idling.
2. Throttle about one-quarter open for running light.
3. Throttle from one-quarter to three-quarters open for general running.
4. Throttle three-quarters to wide open for full power.

FIG. 14. CARBURETTOR

1. Air cleaner.
2. Tapering needle.
3. Control wire adjuster.
4. Submerged main jet
5. Float.
6. Tickler.

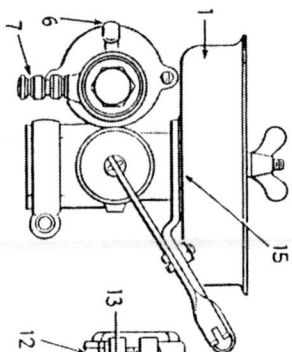

7. Fuel supply pipe fixing stub.
8. Mixing chamber cover.
9. Fuel filler.
10. Throttle slide.
11. Jet spray nozzle.
12. Collar tightening screw.

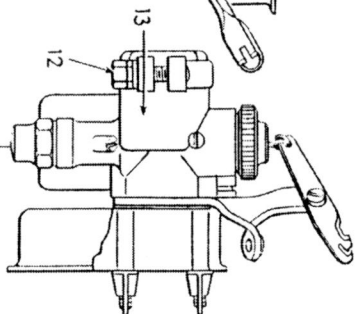

13. Mixing chamber.
14. Hinged control arm.
15. Choke control plate.
16. Main jet plug.
17. Fixed abutment.

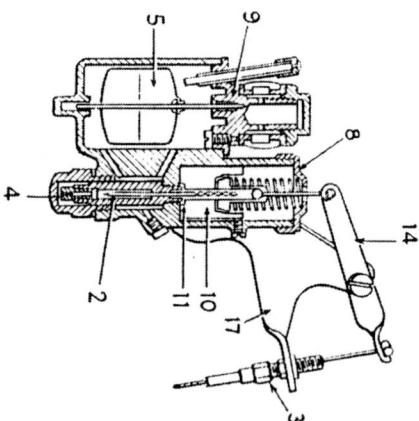

With the engine warmed up, start tuning the carburettor in this order. FIRST OPERATION (Section 4). Use the smallest main jet that will give full power when running under load on the level. If the engine runs slightly better with the throttle not quite wide open, the jet is just right for economy, but on the small side for those who habitually intend to use full power.

SECOND OPERATION (Section 3). Set the needle position as low as possible in relation to good acceleration and running at half throttle. "Spitting"

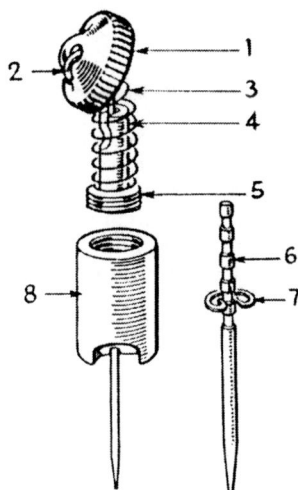

FIG. 15. CARBURETTOR: THROTTLE AND TAPERING NEEDLE

1. Mixing chamber cover.
2. Ball end control lever.
3. Throttle slide spring.
4. Slide operating shaft.
5. Threaded needle clip anchor.
6. Tapering needle.
7. Needle position clip.
8. Throttle slide.

in the carburettor on acceleration means the mixture is too weak; raise the needle one groove at a time.

THIRD OPERATION (Sections 2 and 1). If the idling mixture at 1 and the take-off at 2 are weak—indicated by the engine spitting and fading out— use a smaller cut-away. If the engine runs lumpily, this indicates a rich mixture at slow speeds. Use a larger cut-away.

GENERAL NOTE

Any change of throttle cut-away may necessitate readjustment of the needle position. A throttle with a smaller cut-away may require the needle lowered, alternatively a larger cut-away may necessitate raising the needle.

Erratic Slow Running, not cured by Adjustment. Erratic slow running is often caused by an air leak at the point of attachment of carburettor to induction pipe, or at the gasket between the induction pipe flange and the cylinder.

TRACING FAULTS

If engine runs with reduced performance, first make sure that there is ample petrol mixture in the fuel tank, good compression, a clean sparking plug and a good spark at the points. It is assumed that the silencer is clean (*see* page 38). Verify complete opening and closing of the throttle and choke plate. See that the air filter is clean.

If all these are in order, check further as follows—

1. If the float chamber floods when tickler is depressed indicating clear fuel supply line, yet the plug points are grey and dry after reasonably hard driving (*see* page 49), this suggests a blockage of the main jet. To remedy, remove the main-jet plug at the base of the mixing chamber, unscrew the main jet and clear the jet orifice by blowing through it.

2. Verify that the carburettor is clean internally, that the drilled passageways are clear and that the main jet and needle jet are screwed up firmly. Ensure that the needle is held in position in the throttle by its clip.

3. If all the above points are in order the only possible carburation faults are in mixture control which can be varied in accordance with instructions in the Tuning section. The following will help to differentiate between RICH and WEAK mixture.

SYMPTOMS OF RICH MIXTURE—

Black sooty exhaust smoke.
Petrol spraying out of air cleaner.
Engine "four-stroking."
Heavy lumpy running.
Heavy petrol consumption.
Sparking plug sooty.

SOME CAUSES FOR ABOVE—

Punctured float, or float needle bent or worn.
Tickler stuck down.
Needle raised too much in the throttle.
Main jet too large, or loose.
Needle jet worn.
Air filter choked.

SYMPTOMS OF WEAK MIXTURE

"Spitting" in the carburettor.
Erratic slow running.
Poor acceleration.
Overheating.
Sparking plug dry grey colour around the points.

SOME CAUSES FOR ABOVE—

Air leaks.

Petrol supply tap not fully open or fuel low in tank.

Jet partially choked.

Impurities in needle guide at floor of float chamber preventing needle lowering completely.

Too small main jet.

Needle too low in the throttle.

Air filter has been removed.

Petrol contains water.

Finally, when the performance at all throttle positions is correct, the adjusting screw at the end of the throttle control arm should be adjusted to obtain slow running with the twist grip control fully closed.

The makers of the carburettor and all the parts relevant to it are Amal Ltd., Holford Road, Witton, Birmingham, 6.

CHAPTER X

THE EXHAUST SYSTEM

THE exhaust pipe and silencer form a one-piece unit with a detachable snubber, held inside the silencer body.

Failure to remove the silencer unit for thorough cleaning at least once

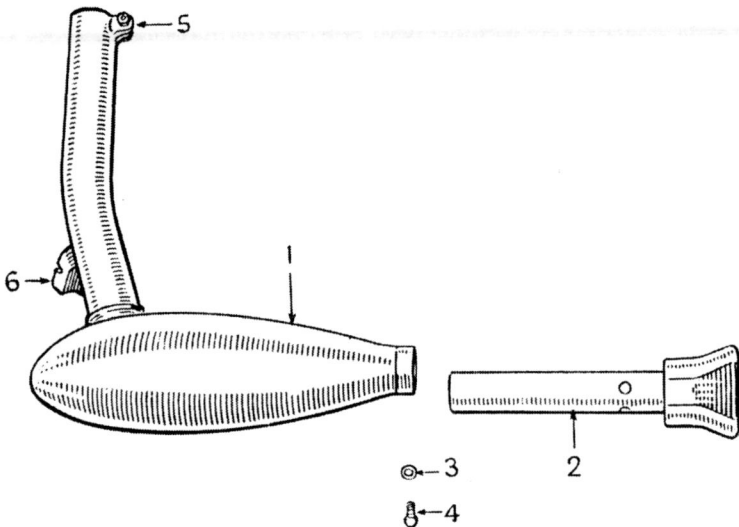

FIG. 16. EXHAUST SILENCER SYSTEM

1. Silencer main body.
2. Detachable snubber.
3. Plain washer.
4. Snubber securing bolt.

5. Exhaust pipe clamp bolt.
6. Bracket for fixing silencer to suspension arm bracket.

every 1,500 miles may result in loss of power, heavy petrol consumption, bad starting and erratic running.

TO REMOVE THE UNIT COMPLETE—

1. Slacken off the pinch-bolt clamping the exhaust pipe to the cylinder, using a long box spanner to reach the nut located between the cylinder barrel and the rear suspension arm.

2. Completely remove the silencer securing-bolt, at the bottom of

the engine bearer-bracket. The silencer unit can now be pulled away from the cylinder. Remove the small bolt, holding the snubber, to the expansion chamber, and withdraw the snubber complete.

Easy Decarbonizing. It is recommended that the silencer and snubber units be left overnight in a bath of "Gunk H.S. Hydro Seal" decarbonizing compound. They will then come spotlessly clean by swishing in hot water, avoiding the tedious and dirty job of scraping which must be done unless "Gunk" is used.

The silencer and snubber can now be reassembled, care being taken to ensure that the end of the snubber mates with its ring inside the expansion chamber. Bolt up carefully, making sure that the locking washer is in position. As a good finish to a job well done, paint the assembly with some good cylinder black.

When dry, return the unit to the machine, smearing a small quantity of graphite grease on the securing bolt threads to ensure easy removal next time. Make the joint at the exhaust pipe clip really tight. Leakage at this joint causes popping and banging when the machine is on the overrun.

Regular attention to this task will increase the period of running between fuller dismantling of the engine for decarbonization and greatly reduces the tendency for the rings to become stuck by gumming in their grooves.

CHAPTER XI

THE ENGINE

MAINTENANCE of the Vespa engine, which has the characteristic simplicity of construction of the two-stroke, should be an easy and straightforward task for the average owner. Adequate instructions for a complete overhaul of the power unit will be found in the following pages.

DECARBONIZING

THE period for "de-coking" the engine is between 3,000 and 4,000 miles, dependent on driving conditions. The need will be shown by the following symptoms—

1. Poor starting.
2. Petrol consumption slightly above average.
3. Erratic acceleration.
4. Poor climbing and loss of power.

For ease of handling it is most desirable to remove the power-unit complete from the machine as described on page 27. The silencer assembly should be dealt with as outlined on page 38.

Before commencing work, obtain the following spares from local Vespa agent—

1. Cylinder base gasket.
2. Induction pipe gasket.
3. Cylinder head copper joint-washer.

(N.B. If the copper head-gasket shows no visible signs of blowing or leaking, indicated by black streak marks on the two faces, it can be used again IF it is first annealed.)

To anneal, the gasket should first be cleaned, heated to a uniform dull red in colour and immediately immersed in CLEAN COLD WATER. It should never be used more than three times in this manner. For the average private owner it is recommended that renewal be made every time the cylinder head is removed. In some cases a "Hallite" gasket has been used for the cylinder head joint. These must always be replaced; copper and "Hallite" gaskets are interchangeable.

When the power unit has been removed from the machine (*see* page 27) all dirt should be cleaned off the gear casing before any further dismantling is carried out. Use only clean petrol or "Gunk" as cleaning material.

Dismantling the Engine. When clean, the unit can be clamped gently but firmly in the vice by the two flat faces provided on the final drive housing, using soft vice jaws. Detach the H.T. cable from the sparking plug and unscrew the plug. Unscrew the nut on the cylinder head fixing the cooling air cowl, remove the locking washer and slip the cowl off its stud.

Unscrew the three cylinder head nuts, taking from each stud, one locking washer and one plain washer. The cylinder head can now be gently separated from and pulled off the cylinder barrel. Using a knife, lever the gasket carefully from the recess in the cylinder barrel.

Crank the kick-starter to bring the piston to the top of the cylinder (T.D.C.). The cylinder barrel can now be pulled from the three long

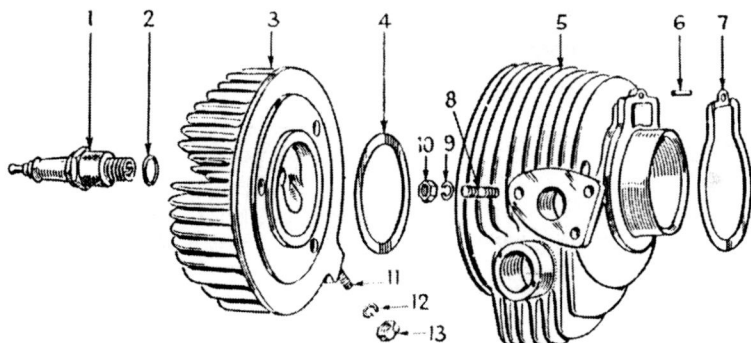

FIG. 17. CYLINDER HEAD AND BARREL

1. Sparking plug.
2. Copper-asbestos plug washer.
3. Cylinder head.
4. Cylinder joint gasket.
5. Cylinder barrel.
6. Locating peg.
7. Base joint washer.
8. Induction pipe stud.
9. Spring washer.
10. Induction pipe nut.
11. Air duct stud.
12. Spring washer.
13. Air duct nut.

crankcase studs. Cover the mouth of the crankcase with clean rag to prevent the possible entry of foreign matter.

Remove the gudgeon-pin circlips (2) using a pair of pointed pliers. Soak a rag in boiling water and, while hot, wrap it round the piston for a few minutes. The gudgeon-pin can then be pushed out of the piston with light pressure, thereby avoiding risk of bending the connecting rod through the use of a punch.

Remove all traces of the old gasket and jointing compound from the face of the crankcase taking care not to damage the face in the process. (An old blunt knife is an ideal tool.)

Getting Rid of Carbon Easily. If the cylinder barrel and head, also the piston with rings are placed in "Gunk" H.S. de-carbonizing compound overnight and washed in warm water the following day, the carbon will wash off as a fluid, obviating much laborious scraping.

Scraping is worth avoiding, not only from the labour aspect, but because of the risk of altering running clearances. The piston and ring grooves are particularly susceptible. Should scraping be done, great care must be taken to remove carbon only from the piston and not metal as well.

Make sure that all traces of carbon are removed from the top of the cylinder barrel, the inlet, exhaust and transfer ports, and remove any traces of old base gasket and jointing compound from the joint face of the cylinder base flange. Similarly check the cylinder head, paying particular attention to the plug threads.

After decarbonizing and ring checking thoroughly clean the barrel, cylinder head, piston and rings in either "Gunk" or petrol. Avoid the use

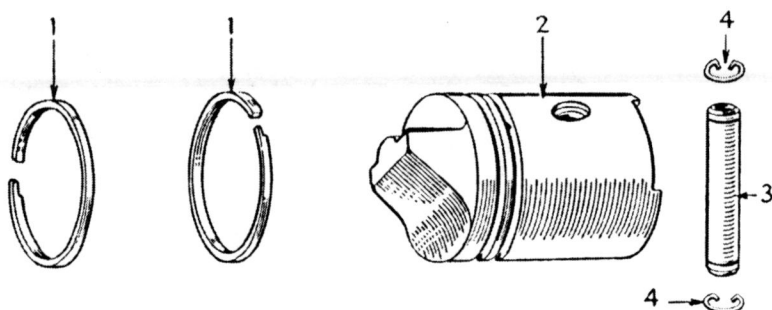

FIG. 18. PISTON ASSEMBLY

1. Piston ring.	3. Gudgeon-pin.
2. Piston.	4. Circlip.

of paraffin which has a corrosive effect on cast iron. When dry, the barrel exterior can be given a light coating of cylinder black.

Care of Piston Rings. If the immersion in "Gunk" procedure is used to clean the piston and ring grooves with rings, the removal of piston rings is simplified. By using three strips of tin 1 in. × ¼ in. slipped between the piston and each ring in turn at approximately 120 degrees distance, the ring can be slipped off the piston without fear of breakage. Avoid straining the rings in any way. (The strips of tin should not have raw edges from cutting with snips.)

To Check the Ring End Gap. Place the clean piston ring approximately 1½ in. inside the cylinder barrel. Insert the piston, bottom end first, to push the ring square in the barrel. Measure the gap between the ends of the ring with feeler gauges. This gap should not be more than 0·008 in. If more, new rings should be fitted. One end only of the new rings should be filed to ensure correct structural detail in the spigot step and the end gap in the case of new rings should be not more than 0·006 in. nor less than 0·004 in.

To Check Vertical Play of the Rings. After all the carbon deposit has been removed from the ring grooves in the piston, the rings should be checked (each in its own groove) for vertical play, again using feeler gauges. The correct clearance is not less than 0·003 in. and not more than 0·005 in. New rings should be eased down on one face only by placing a piece of emery sheet on a surface plate or piece of ground sheet glass and gently rubbing the ring down with a circular movement.

Reassembly. Warm the piston (less rings) for a few moments in boiling water, position it correctly over the small end and push the gudgeon-pin home while still warm, making sure the piston is the correct way up. The sloping part of the piston goes to the top side of the engine. Replace the circlips. When the piston is cool, replace the rings in the piston ring grooves, and lightly smear graphite grease or clean engine oil over the whole bearing area of the piston but not the head. Remove the rag from the crankcase mouth.

Lightly cover each side of the cylinder-base gasket with jointing compound and place it on the base of the cylinder barrel. Make sure that the peg in the cylinder barrel has not been disturbed. By gently easing the cylinder barrel on to the top land of the piston, the rings can be compressed into the barrel providing that the end gap of the ring lines up with the spigot pins in the ring groove. Slide the cylinder barrel down the piston, and three studs on to the crankcase face.

Place the cylinder head gasket in the recess of the cylinder barrel, replace the cylinder head and on each cylinder stud place one plain washer, one locking washer and one nut. Screw each nut down equally until all are tight.

Replace the sparking plug (see Section 5). If the old one is being used again, a new C. & A. washer is advised. Avoid over-tightening which may damage the threads in the alloy cylinder head. Replace the H.T. cable and the power unit is ready for bolting on to the rear suspension arm.

After positioning, refit the induction pipe, using a new gasket (no jointing compound). The nuts, each with a locking washer, should be tightened down evenly.

Replace the silencer, tighten the clamping ring on the exhaust port and, before replacing the rear wheel, run the engine for a few moments to allow the unit to warm up. When warm, stop the engine and check the cylinder head and induction pipe nuts and the silencer ring nut. All may be found to need a little more tightening.

Replace the cooling air cowl with lock washer and nut.

Replace the rear wheel and adjust its brake. Check the oil level in the gear case and top-up, or replenish as necessary (see page 69).

If new piston rings have been fitted, run in carefully for approximately 250 miles.

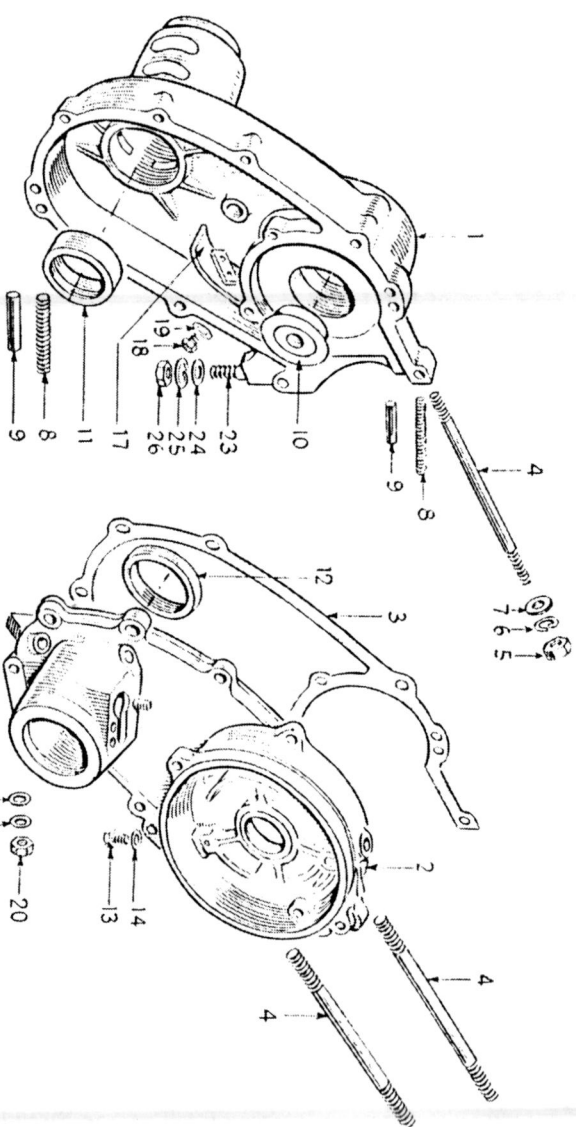

FIG. 19. CRANKCASE

1. Crankcase-half clutch-side.
2. Crankcase-half magneto-side.
3. Joint face gasket.
4. Cylinder and head stud.
5. Cylinder head nut.
6. Cylinder head spring washer.
7. Cylinder head plain washer.

8. Crankcase joint stud.
9. Crankcase positioning dowel.
10. Crankcase oil seal.
11. Bearing housing.
12. Bearing ring.
13. Crankcase drain plug.
14. Crankcase drain plug washer.

15. Oil level plug.
16. Fibre washer.
17. Oil drip-tray.
18. Tray securing bolt.
19. Copper washer.
20. Crankcase joint securing nut.
21. Spring washer.

22. Plain washer.
23. Engine steady-stud.
24. Plain washer.
25. Spring washer.
26. Engine steady-nut.

DISMANTLING THE COMBINED CRANKCASE AND GEAR CASE

The gear case cannot be dismantled until the flywheel generator (page 60), clutch assembly (page 50), cylinder barrel and piston (Section 1) have been removed. Drain the gear case oil from the clutch housing recess—its cover is held by three screws.

The crank and gear case is split down the centre of the big end and the halves are bolted together by twelve studs, each with a nut, a locking washer and a plain washer on the flywheel generator side.

Move the gear-change bell-crank into top gear and unscrew two screws holding the bell-crank plate. The plate, with bell-crank complete can then be removed by depressing the kick-starter lever slightly and gently pulling the crank arm out of the hole thus exposed.

Remove the two bolts with lock washers, holding the kick-starter lever to its boss. Remove the lever and dust seal plate and felt oil seal thus exposed.

Unscrew the locking nut and bolt positioning the kick-starter release ring. The bolt may be removed entirely but this is unnecessary.

Splitting the Case. Remove the flywheel generator (*see* page 61), remove the spring circlip from the generator flywheel and take out the centre fixing nut. Screw this on to the flywheel side crankshaft thread. To avoid possible damage to the crankshaft, a piece of flat steel of exact width should be inserted between the crank webs directly opposite to the crankpin to steady the assembly. By tapping with a hide hammer first the nut on the crankshaft then the kick-starter fixing boss, the gear case will come apart, the main ball races remaining on the shafts. When the flywheel side case is detached, remove the fixing nut and return it to the flywheel, replacing the circlip (ensure correct entry in the groove in flywheel).

Remove the clutch assembly (*see* page 50), similarly screw the serrated clutch nut on to the clutch shaft and gently tap the crankshaft out of the gear casing.

Crankshaft Repairs. Owing to the need for extreme accuracy required in reassembling the crankshaft and main bearings it is advisable at least to hand the crankshaft to your agent with instructions to replace main, big-end or small-end bearings. In fact, the whole of the work in this section should only be undertaken by a skilled engineer.

The flywheels or crank webs should be true when reassembled, for as little error as 0·001 in. will seriously affect the smooth running and will soon damage the main bearings and their respective housings.

Big-end and bearing over-size parts are supplied by the makers in two sizes listed hereunder.

Attempts at private grinding of the crankpin, connecting rod big-end, or the crank webs should under NO circumstances be undertaken. Such work will seriously affect the hardened surfaces.

OVERSIZE PARTS

OVERSIZE CRANK-PIN
1st Oversize	.	.	.	. 21·20 ± 0·01 mm.
2nd Oversize	.	.	.	. 21·30 ± 0·01 mm.

OVERSIZE CONNECTING ROD BIG-END
1st Oversize	.	.	.	. 33·18 ± 0·02 mm.
2nd Oversize	.	.	.	. 33·28 ± 0·02 mm.

OVERSIZE BORE IN CRANK WEBS
1st Oversize	.	.	.	. 21·00 ± 0·003 mm.
2nd Oversize	.	.	.	. 21·10 ± 0·003 mm.

REASSEMBLY

While the crankshaft is being attended to, use a blunt knife to remove all traces of old face gasket and jointing compound from the crank and gear case joints, paying special attention to the roots of the studs.

Examine the main bearing oil seals for—

1. Failure of the spring.
2. Breakdown of the rubber compound.
3. Signs of scrubbing (indicated by shiny patches on the seal faces) caused by too thick an oil seal. There should be 0·003 in. crankshaft side-float when erected.

To rectify, the oil seal should be pressed out of the crankcase and eased down on a sheet of fine emery cloth until all signs of scrub marks are eradicated. THOROUGHLY clean it in petrol and allow to dry. Do not return the seals to the crankcase.

When all the parts are clean, assembly should be carried out in this order. Place on each axle of the crankshaft one main bearing, one oil seal, flange side to main bearing. Heat the clutch side of the gearcase in boiling water and push the clutch side mainshaft, complete with oil seal and main bearing, into the housing. The crankcase must be heated as damage to the gear case will result if the bearings are forced in. Check that the axle and bearing are right home and correctly in position.

Place the gear case half in a vice with soft jaws, clamping on the two flats on the final drive case; the gear cluster should be placed in position (*see* page 54), avoiding excessive pressure. Check that the small kick-starter actuating springs have ⅛ in. free length. If less, new springs must be fitted. Use grease to stick the two springs in their respective holes in the kick-starter boss and place the boss in position on the kick-starter ratchet gear and release ring assembly already mounted on the cross guide bush (page 59). Engage the return spring into the smaller of the two slots cut in the release ring; a piece of copper-wire will assist in pulling the spring into position.

Remove the rubber sealing ring (which should be replaced if damaged

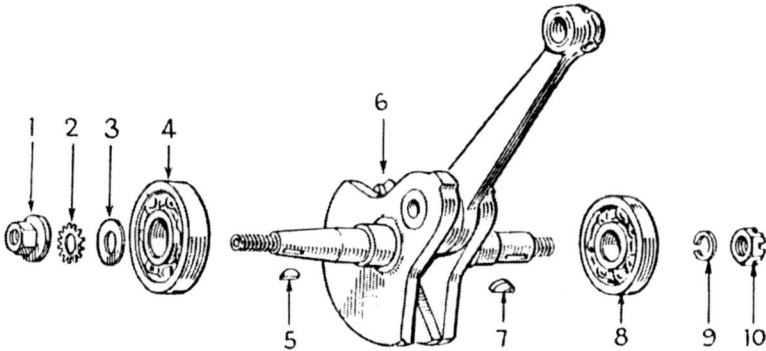

FIG. 20. CRANKSHAFT

1. Flywheel magneto extractor-nut.
2. Lock washer.
3. Plain washer.
4. Main bearing.
5. Flywheel key.

6. Crankshaft assembly.
7. Clutch key.
8. Main bearing.
9. Spring washer.
10. Clutch nut.

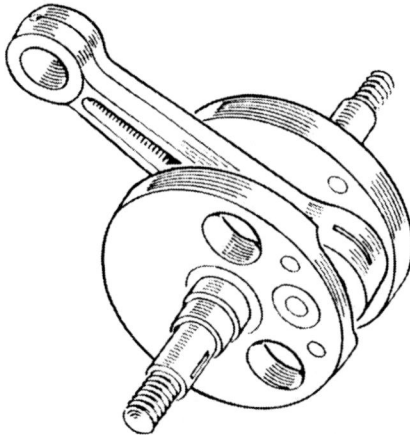

FIG. 21. 1955 TYPE CRANKSHAFT

A crankshaft of new design has been introduced for 1955. The main bearings have been increased in size and the big end of the connecting-rod is of larger section.

from the kick-starter housing in the flywheel-side case, and place it on the step of the kick-starter boss.

Smear jointing compound lightly on both sides of the crankcase gasket and place the gasket in position on the gear case half held in the vice.

Heat the flywheel generator side half-case in boiling water and the half-case will fall into position on the crankshaft bearing and kick-starter assembly. Bolt up the twelve studs, plain washer to case, then locking washer and then nut. Tighten the nuts evenly until the whole is tight.

DO NOT place any locking washers directly against the alloy casing or damage will result. When all nuts are firmly tightened, spin the flywheel

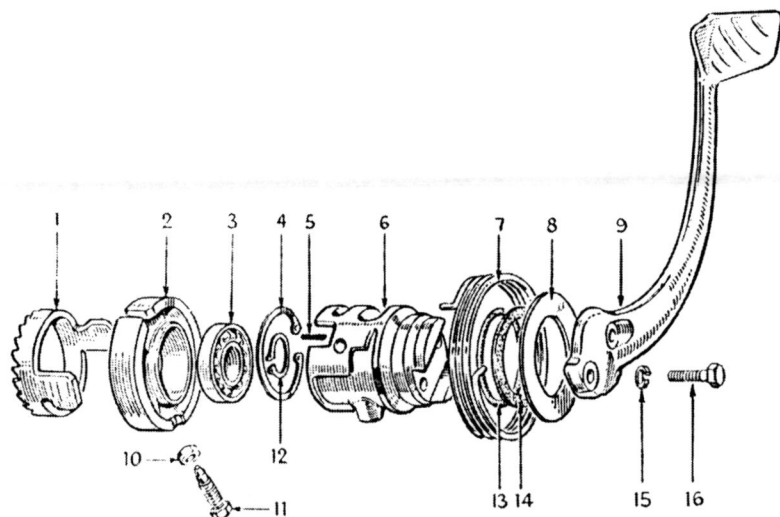

FIG. 22. KICKSTART GROUP

1. Ratchet gear ring.	9. Kick-start pedal.
2. Bearing housing.	10. Lock-nut.
3. Bearing.	11. Bearing housing locking bolt.
4. Bearing securing circlip.	12. Bearing circlip.
5. Ratchet actuating spring.	13. Rubber sealing ring.
6. Kick-start main body.	14. Felt sealing washer.
7. Return spring.	15. Spring washer.
8. Dust seal washer.	16. Kick-start pedal securing bolt.

axle to test for free rotation. Should the crankshaft be tight, tap the end of the clutch-side axle with a slight inward blow with a hide hammer. This has the effect of centralizing the flywheel generator axle bearing.

Place the kick-starter lever on its boss and screw in one stud, depress the lever until the large slot cut in the release ring corresponds with the locking bolt hole, screw in the locking bolt until the release ring is held and then lock it in position with the lock-nut.

Press the kick-starter lever down until the hole in the actuating boss allows the gear-change bell-crank to be slipped into the selector-rod groove. When correctly positioned replace the two bell-crank plate holding screws.

Test the kick-starter for correct engagement and release.

By turning the final drive shaft operate the gear selector-rod to check correct engagement of the gears. Replace the clutch (page 52), flywheel generator (page 60), piston, cylinder barrel and head (Section 1) and reassemble the power unit in the machine.

Remove the kick-starter lever and replace the felt seal and dust washer, place the kick-starter lever in position and tighten the two holding bolts (one locking washer to each bolt). Refill the gear case to the correct level with Castrol XL oil, replacing the inspection-hole plug with a fibre washer.

If main, big-end, or small-end bearings have been replaced, the machine should be run carefully for the first 500 miles. In the case of big-end, or main bearings being renewed the oil should be increased in the petrol to the correct running-in amount ($\frac{2}{3}$ pint Castrol XL to 1 gal. petrol).

SPARKING PLUGS

At regular intervals of 2,000 miles or at each decarbonizing period it is advisable to have the sparking plug cleaned and tested at the local agent.

In the event of the plug being damaged or worn beyond further efficient use, do not hesitate to scrap it and replace it with a new one. On no account keep such discarded plugs as "spares for an emergency" as considerable damage can result from their continued use.

The following recommendations should ensure maximum satisfaction.

SPARKING PLUG RECOMMENDATION

(Sparking plug sizes 14 mm. thread short reach.)

For short daily journeys the writer recommends that the following plugs should be used—

Lodge	C.N.
K.L.G.	F.50
Champion (English)	L.10
Bosch	W.175/T1
Marelli	C.W.175.A.

For journeys entailing hard driving, i.e. touring, use the following plugs—

Lodge	H.H.14
K.L.G.	F.70
Champion (English)	L.10.S.
Bosch	W.225
Marelli	C.W.225.A.

For special work such as competition riding and racing, special plugs are manufactured and the plug manufacturers should be contacted in this respect. The engine and the use to which it is to be put must of course be explained.

CHAPTER XII

THE CLUTCH

To dismantle the clutch, first remove the power unit from the machine (*see* page 27). Thoroughly clean the exterior of the gear casing. The clutch is on the crankshaft opposite to the flywheel generator. Unscrew the three securing screws and remove the clutch housing cover. Should the cover be in any way tight in the casing, operate the clutch release lever and this will force them apart.

The clutch body is thus exposed and, by tilting the engine unit, the oil in the gear case can be drained out. Remove the clutch pressure plate before unscrewing the serrated clutch-centre nut. Stand the engine unit on its cylinder head before starting to remove the clutch body in order to eliminate the possibility of the needle rollers falling into the gear case. Then, with a stout screwdriver or flat bar holding the clutch body through one of its slots, unscrew the clutch nut with the special castellated box spanner. Remove the locking washer and pull the clutch body off the mainshaft. When pulling the clutch body off the mainshaft, the twenty-nine needle rollers on which the clutch drive gear is supported are free to fall out. Check that all are recovered before proceeding further.

To Dismantle the Clutch. Having secured all needle rollers, place the clutch body complete with the drive gear in the vice so that one jaw presses on the end of the drive gear and the other presses on a plate resting on all the spring cups. By tightening gently this will relieve spring pressure from the clutch body and will free the large spring circlip in the back of the clutch body. Remove this circlip and, by gently releasing the vice, the clutch body can be removed. Remove the clutch plates in this order—

1. Bearing plate.
2. Friction plate.
3. Bearing plate.
4. Friction plate.
5. Main clutch bearing plate.

This will leave the clutch body and six clutch springs. The six spring retaining cups are a press fit in the clutch body.

The parts can then be washed in clean petrol and when dry examined in this order—

1. FRICTION PLATES. Check that each friction plate is complete with eighteen large and eighteen small corks, that the corks are in no way damaged and that they are between $\frac{5}{32}$ in. and $\frac{3}{16}$ in. thick. Should there

be any shiny marks on the steel surfaces of the friction plate, new cork inserts will be required. (On some machines two teeth are missing from each friction plate; this is in order.)

2. BEARING PLATES. Check for truth and flatness. Blue colour marks on

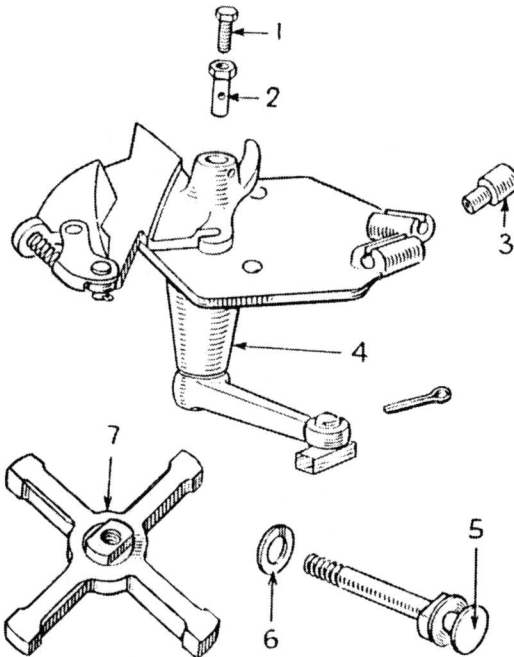

FIG. 23. 1955 TYPE GEAR SELECTOR DETAILS

1. Operating cable pinch-bolt.
2. Operating cable anchor.
3. Cable end ferrule.
4. Cable operated selector plate.
5. Selector-spindle.
6. Plain washer.
7. Selector-spider.

Gear selection on the 1955 type Vespa is now operated by a system of pull cables. The selector spider is screwed on to the selector-spindle superseding the use of a rivet. The method of dismantling the gear case, however, remains the same.

one edge suggest that the plate is bent and may require renewal. A uniform shiny bearing area is required. Under NO circumstances should the bearing plates be roughened. Smooth surfaces do NOT cause clutch slip.

3. CLUTCH SPRINGS. The correct length of the springs is one inch. If less than $\frac{7}{8}$ in. long, replace them. Any springs bent or twisted should be replaced.

To Re-line the Clutch. Materials required for re-lining the clutch are—

36 large corks | Stocked by the local
36 small corks | Vespa Agent.

Press out the old corks from the two friction plates, thoroughly clean the plates with petrol, and dry.

Place the new corks in boiling water (they will shrink but will return to their original size when dry). Press the new corks, whilst still hot, into the plate. An equal amount of cork should protrude on each side of the plate. When the plates are full the corks should be dried.

Rub each side of the corked plates on a flat sheet of glass paper until the corks are just over ⅛ in. thick with a flat uniform surface. Lightly smear clean Castrol XL over the corks and bearing plates.

Reassembly. Place the six spring-cups into the clutch body and stick with grease, one spring into each cup. Place the main bearing plate on top of the clutch springs ensuring that each spring enters its recess.

Replace the plates in this order—

1. Friction plate.
2. Bearing plate.
3. Friction plate.
4. Bearing plate.

Position the drive gear into the plates and grip the whole in the vice (as dismantled), gently compress the clutch and replace the large circlip into the recess of the clutch body.

After re-lining, the clutch will settle down slightly after approximately 250 miles. The cable adjustment should be checked and adjusted as necessary, after this period.

Fierce Clutch Operation after Reassembly. The only cause of fierce clutch take-up is a faulty clutch pressure plate assembly. (On pre-1955 machines only.) The pin must be tight in the pressure plate. If it is loose the most satisfactory solution is renewal of the assembly. Brazing the pin in usually effects a repair.

An emergency repair can be made if the pressure pin is held in the vice by means of the flats on its long, smaller, *diameter.* Gently tap the head of the pin just enough to tighten the spindle to the plate; avoid heavy blows. This will cure the trouble but the job requires care and unless the owner is a mechanic he would be better advised to obtain new parts. The 1955 modified clutch pressure-plate has no pin but is held with a spring clip.

Clutch Operating Mechanism. If the actuating arm should stick in the event of oil leakage, remove the clutch housing cover as described and proceed as follows—

1. Remove carefully the clutch housing cover sealing ring. (This

sealing ring, of indestructible rubber, should last indefinitely. If damaged through mishandling, replace with a new one.)

2. Remove from the centre boss inside the clutch housing cover the clutch thrust pad.

3. Remove the split-pin and plain washer from the end of the actuating arm shaft.

4. Pull the actuating arm downwards, out of the fulcrum-rod and guide hole.

The return spring is in this way released as is the rubber sealing ring on the actuating arm shaft.

Thoroughly clean (petrol or "Gunk" only) all the parts and reassemble in the following order when dry.

1. Place on the actuating arm shaft the return spring and the rubber sealing ring. Push the bent end of the spring into the hole in the lever.

2. Put a little Castrol XL on the actuating arm shaft and, after placing the fulcrum-rod in the boss of the clutch housing cover, feed the actuating arm shaft through the guide hole and fulcrum-rod.

3. Replace the plain washer to the end of the actuating shaft using a new split-pin.

4. Place the hooked end of the return spring in the cut-away portion of the clutch cover and test the actuating arm for correct movement and return. Should the shaft be tight in the guide hole, it may be gently eased down with fine emery cloth. Before doing this, make certain that it is not binding through dirt or bad fitting (through a broken down oil seal). Afterwards, thoroughly clean with petrol before repeating the above assembly instructions. ON NO ACCOUNT enlarge the hole in the cover plate.

5. Smear graphite grease on the clutch thrust pad and replace the pad in the boss on the fulcrum-rod.

6. Place the sealing ring on the clutch housing cover joint face, fit the cover plate on to the gear casing and thoroughly tighten the three screws.

7. Finally, test the actuating arm to see that the clutch operation works before returning the unit to the machine.

When the unit is once more in the machine, fill the gear casing with Castrol XL to the correct level and adjust the clutch operating cable.

CHAPTER XIII

GEARS AND TRANSMISSION

THE clutch and gears of the Douglas Vespa are all contained in the light alloy gear case. There are no chains. The only maintenence required is regular attention to the oil level in the gear case. If the gear case is dismantled, it will most probably be on account of need for attention to the lower part of the engine.

Motion from the crankshaft is transmitted direct through the clutch to the clutch drive gear (*see* page 55), which engages on the spring-loaded gear forming part of the multiple gear group on the layshaft.

This spring-loaded gear is made in two concentric parts—

1. The outside helical gear rim.

2. A central drive member, fixed to the layshaft which carries three gear wheels meshing with the three-speed gear wheels on the final drive shaft.

The two parts of the spring-loaded gear are connected by twelve small springs (held in place by two steel plates riveted together) which cushion transmission jerks, either driving or on overrun.

The three-speed gears on the final drive shaft rotate freely, but can each in turn be locked for driving, by the gear shift mechanism controlled by the twist-grip on the left handlebar.

The layshaft runs on a ball-roller bearing and needle rollers and is splash lubricated from a drip tray fixed to the gear casing.

The final drive shaft runs on two ball-roller bearings, separated by a tubular distance piece, and located in the final drive tunnel of the gear casing. Between the outer ball race and the end of the final drive tunnel a spring wire distance piece is used to locate this race and the final drive oil seal against the wheel drive flange. For the sizes and number of bearings, needle rollers, etc., see the technical data sheets (page 76).

The Spring-loaded Gear. This requires a special jig for easy and correct replacement of the springs in the rare event of trouble. Owners are strongly advised to return the power unit. If, however, it is intended to remove the gear, proceed as follows. Remove the power unit from the machine (page 27), dismantle the gear case (page 44), remove the kick-starter mechanism as already described, and, by using a BRASS punch from the road wheel end, the final drive shaft and three-speed gears can be gently tapped out of the final drive bearings. Unscrew the layshaft retaining nut and remove the locking and plain washer (some models have a plain washer and

54

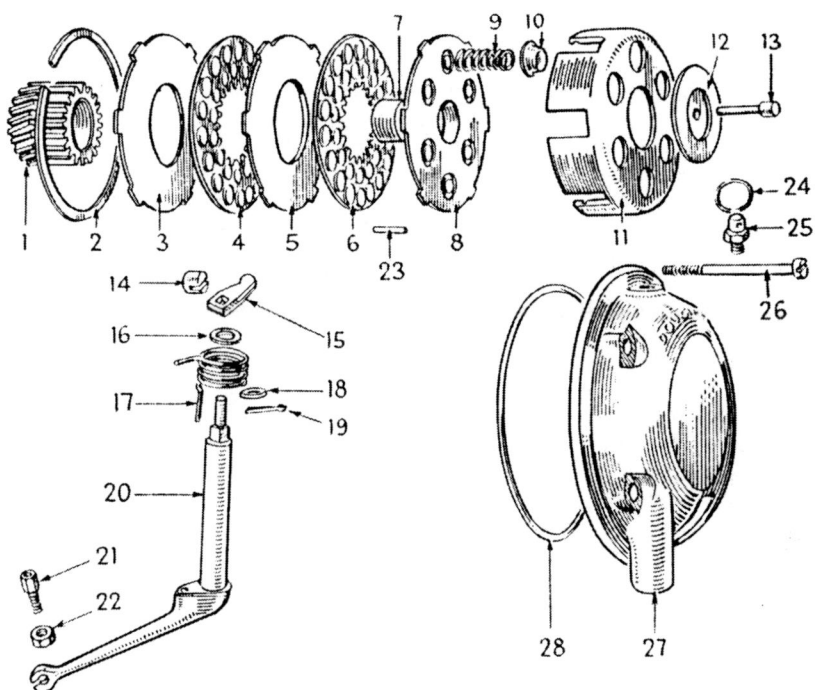

FIG. 24. CLUTCH

1. Clutch drive gear.	15. Actuating bell-crank.
2. Clutch plate securing circlip.	16. Rubber seal ring.
3. Steel drive plate.	17. Return spring.
4. Cork friction plate.	18. Plain washer.
5. Steel drive plate.	19. Split-pin.
6. Cork friction plate.	20. Actuating arm.
7. Needle roller track.	21. Cable adjusting screw.
8. Clutch backplate	22. Lock-nut.
9. Clutch spring.	23. Needle roller.
10. Spring cup.	24. Breather ring.
11. Clutch body.	25. Gear case breather.
12. Pressure plate.	26. Clutch cover screw.
13. Pressure pin.	27. Clutch cover.
14. Actuating pad.	28. Rubber ring seal.

For 1955 a three friction plate clutch was introduced and the pressure plate (12) and pressure pin (13) were superseded by a spring-clip-held pressure plate. This 1955 clutch will fit all Douglas Vespa models but a new clutch cover (27) must also be used.

split-pin). The layshaft retaining nut is outside the gear case and is the only one on the external side of the clutch half-casing.

With a BRASS punch, tap the layshaft out of the casing and the layshaft gear group can then be removed from the layshaft. Before reassembling the gear group on the layshaft, the needle rollers should be examined and replaced if they are in any way damaged. The ball-roller bearing is held in position by a spring circlip in the inner driven member of the spring-loaded gear. Unless it is to be replaced, this bearing can be washed out and oiled in position.

A flat surface on the layshaft can be held in a vice should the layshaft retaining nut have become stiff and difficult to undo or tighten.

To Reassemble the Layshaft Gear Group. If the ball-roller bearing has been removed push it into the inner member of the spring-loaded gear and replace the circlip, ensuring correct entry into the groove provided. Stick the needle rollers on to the seating of the layshaft, using Castrolease (heavy) grease as an adhesive medium. Push the layshaft into the gear group, taking care that no needle rollers are dislodged in the process. The layshaft can be returned to the gear case and the layshaft retaining nut, with plain washer and locking washer, tightened. This must be very firm to lock the shaft permanently for after use. If it is a castellated nut, use a new split-pin.

It may be found in some cases, that the oil drip tray has to be removed to allow the gear cluster to pass the clutch housing. Two bolts only hold the drip tray in position. Each has a copper ring between the head and the gear case. Always renew these copper rings on removal or oil leakage will develop. *Take special note* that the drip tray bolts *must* be tight or the tray may become dislodged with drastic results to the gears. You are strongly recommended to drill a hole in each bolt head and firmly wire the two bolts together when they are finally tightened.

Final Drive Gears. Dismantle the three-speed gear wheels as follows— With the final drive shaft and gear wheels removed from the gear casing as described above, remove the kick-starter gear bearing from the gear cross guide bush and plate. This is done by gently easing off the spring circlip retaining the ball-roller bearing and prising the bearing away from the cross guide bush plate, at the same time drawing the kick-starter return ratchet away.

The cross guide bush and plate is held to the final drive shaft with four bolts with tab lock washers which must always be renewed when reassembling. When the four bolts are removed the cross guide bush and plate can be pulled off, releasing the three gear wheels.

Final Drive Bearings. The inner final drive shaft bearing is held in the final drive tunnel with a screwed ring. With this ring removed, the bearing can be gently tapped out with a long punch, using great care to avoid tilting the bearing and so damaging the housing.

The outer bearing and oil seal are punched out from the opposite end of the tunnel. Do not lose the distance ring between the oil seal and the outer bearing (*see* page 58).

To Reassemble. First make sure that all parts are thoroughly cleaned. Place the inner bearing into the housing (warming the case facilitates correct entry) and tighten home the screwed locking ring.

Place the distance tube into the final drive tunnel and replace the outer bearing, followed by the wire distance ring and oil seal. (N.B. The outer

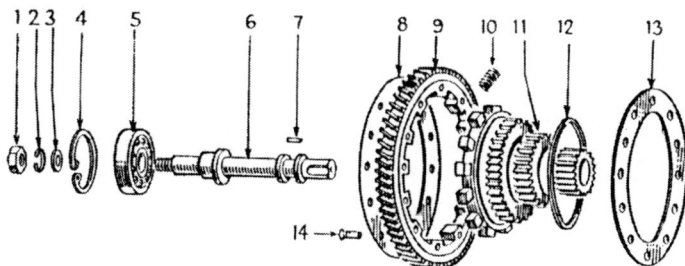

FIG. 25. SPRING GEAR

1. Layshaft securing nut.
2. Layshaft nut spring washer.
3. Plain washer.
4. Layshaft bearing circlip.
5. Layshaft bearing.
6. Spring gear layshaft.
7. Layshaft needle rollers.

8. Inner spring retaining plate
9. Outer gear rim.
10. Cush drive spring.
11. Layshaft gear cluster.
12. Spacing ring.
13. Outer spring retaining plate.
14. Retaining plates securing rivet.

bearing differs from the inner one in that its bearing track is completely filled with balls. The inner bearing has a brass spacer between each ball.) Before reassembling the three-speed gears and the final drive shaft, check the following points.

(*a*) Gear wheel teeth free from chips, etc.

(*b*) Kick-starter teeth on large gear wheel not rounded or damaged.

(*c*) Gear selector-cross edges perfectly square.

(*d*) Guide bush and guide rod not unduly worn.

If O.K. place on the final drive shaft in the following order—

1. Small gear wheel (top gear).

2. Medium gear wheel (second gear).

3. Large gear wheel (bottom gear).

4. Cross guide bush and plate.

Finally tighten the four holding bolts with a NEW tab-washer to each bolt. Before turning the tabs of the locking washers, the gear selector-rod and cross should be tested for free sliding through the three gear wheels.

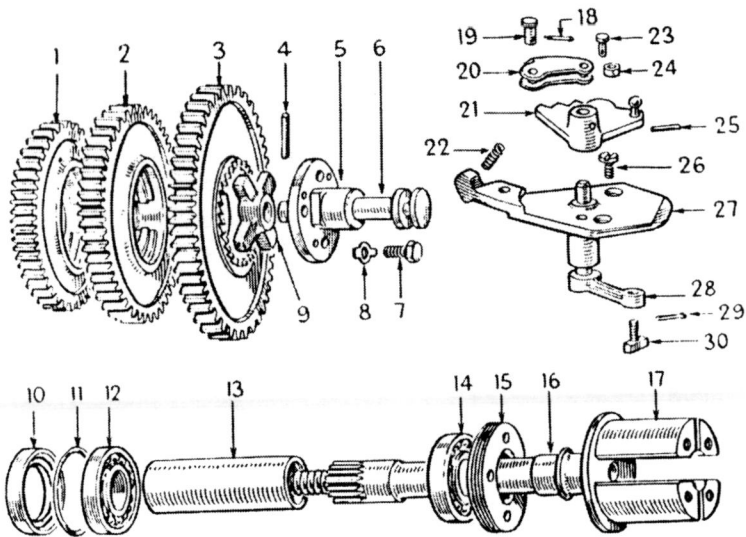

FIG. 26. GEAR GROUP

1. Top gear.
2. Second gear.
3. Bottom gear.
4. Cross securing pin.
5. Cross spindle guide bush.
6. Cross spindle.
7. Guide bush securing bolt.
8. Locking tab-washer.
9. Selector-cross.
10. Rear wheel oil seal.
11. Spring distance ring.
12. Bearing.
13. Spacer-tube.
14. Bearing.
15. Screwed bearing securing ring.
16. Final drive shaft.
17. Ground track for gear wheels.
18. Split-pin.
19. Clevis pin.
20. Spring plate.
21. Selector plate.
22. Stop spring.
23. Clevis pin.
24. Roller.
25. Bell-crank securing rivet.
26. Guide plate securing screw.
27. Selector guide plate.
28. Selector bell-crank.
29. Split-pin.
30. "T" piece.

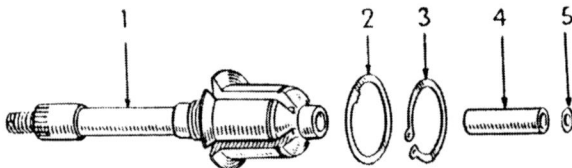

FIG. 27. 1955 FINAL DRIVE SHAFT

1. Final drive shaft.
2. Spacing shim.
3. Gear securing circlip.
4. Spindle guide bush.
5. Plain washer.

Correct gear alignment is now obtained by using spacing shims (No. 2) of varying thicknesses.

The final drive shaft and gears can then be replaced in the bearings, at the same time ensuring that the gear wheels mesh correctly with the layshaft gears.

Finally replace on the cross guide bush plate in this order—
1. Kick-starter ratchet and release ring.
2. Kick-starter bearing.
3. Bearing retaining circlip.

Complete assembly of the kick-starter gears and gear case as outlined on pages 46–9.

COMMON FAULTS AND THEIR REMEDIES

KICK-STARTER FAILS TO MESH CORRECTLY.

1. Kick-starter gear wheel and ratchet damaged.
Remedy: replace the damaged parts.
2. Kick-starter actuating springs damaged or too short.
Remedy: replace—on no account try to effect a cure by pulling the springs longer.

MACHINE JUMPS OUT OF GEAR

1. Inner teeth of gear wheels damaged or broken.
Remedy: renew.
2. Cross guide bush and plate allows excessive end play on the wheels. (The gear wheels should be free to revolve but should have no perceptible end-float.)
Remedy: remove the cross guide bush and plate and turn off in a lathe a small cutting on the FINAL drive shaft bearing surface of the cross guide, bush and plate.
3. Selector-cross, worn.
Remedy: renew. (To remove the selector-cross use a small nail punch to knock the rivet out of the centre of the cross and push the shaft out of the cross centre. Refit with a new rivet.)

MACHINE JUMPS OUT OF TOP GEAR ONLY

Selector-cross not engaging the top gear correctly.
Remedy: shim the final drive shaft between the gear stop ridge and the inner roller bearing to bring the gears into the centre of the case.

It must be emphasized that when remedying any of the above faults only a small amount of turning or shimming is done at a time, otherwise irreparable damage may be caused to the gears or gear case. The work should only be attempted by experienced mechanics.

CHAPTER XIV

THE FLYWHEEL GENERATOR

THE generator unit is made up of two parts, a flywheel and a backplate.

Flywheel. This comprises six permanent magnets and pole pieces round which is cast an aluminium body. A steel hub, with an internal taper and key-way to fit the engine mainshaft, is riveted to the aluminium body. The hub is formed as a cam to operate the contact-breaker rocker arm.

Backplate. This bolts on to the main engine casing and holds the essentials for lighting and ignition—
(a) Two lighting coils.
(b) Ignition coil.
(c) Contact-breaker mechanism.
(d) Condenser.
The screw threads on this unit are not to British standards. Replacements should, therefore, be obtained from the manufacturers or their appointed service agents.

The Flywheel's Magnetism. The flywheel can be removed from the backplate without loss of magnetism but should not be separated from the backplate longer than necessary. It is advisable to ensure that the flywheel is placed on a clean surface and NOT where it is liable to attract iron or steel swarf or filings.

Piaggio Generators. In some machines these Italian units are fitted. All parts are similar to those on the B.T.-H. units, the only difference being the setting of contact-point gap.

MAINTENANCE

The unit requires the minimum of attention. The following, which should be checked every 1,500 miles or during engine overhauls, will keep the unit in first class condition.

Contact Gap. Check the contact gap and adjust to the following exact gaps using a feeler gauge—

> B.T.-H. . . . 0·012 in.
> PIAGGIO . . . 0·016 in.

The large holes in the flywheel are so positioned that one hole shows the contact points just opening, the other shows them fully open. Adjust to the latter hole only.

Lubrication. Use ONLY Castrolease (heavy) grease for lubricating the two points of the unit.
Viz: 1. Rocker-arm pivot-pin.
     2. Cam lubricating pad.
A thin film of grease is all that is required; excess may find its way on to the contact points.

Removal of Unit from Engine. Raise the engine cowl and secure it at its fullest extent.

Remove the air cowl from the cylinder barrel by unscrewing the single fixing nut and remove the locking washer, then pull the air channel off the cylinder barrel stud. Remove the H.T. cable from the spark plug terminal and pick-up assembly (*see* page 40). Unscrew the pick-up assembly, beneath which is a felt ring. Renew the felt ring if it is contaminated as this is the easiest means of H.T. current leakage.

Remove the impeller grid (five holding screws).

Prise the inspection plate spring clip from the groove in the fan body and remove the inspection plate. Hold the flywheel and fan assembly and unscrew the centre fixing nut. A spring circlip, retained in a groove in the cam body, acts as a puller. When the centre nut is unscrewed, its shoulder presses against this circlip so pulling the flywheel off the tapered mainshaft.

To Remove the Backplate. With the flywheel removed scribe marks on the backplate and gear casing to ensure reassembly with the same ignition timing.

Remove the L.T. current cables from the terminal block by unscrewing the fixing screws (2) and remove the locking washers. Remove the terminal clips (3) from the cable ends, using a soldering iron, and unscrew the terminal block, feeding the L.T. cables through the block at the same time (avoid twisting the cables). Another felt washer is placed underneath the terminal block. This also should be replaced if contaminated. Unscrew the backplate holding screws (3) and remove the locking washer and plain washer from each screw.

The backplate can then be gently pulled off the housing of the gear casing, any oil or grease in the housing should be cleaned off using clean petrol.

Should the need for replacement of the H.T. coil or L.T. coils arise, great care must be exercised when fitting the replacement parts. To ensure that the flywheel does not foul the pole tips, ALWAYS press the coil assembly inwards when tightening the screws. There are two screws to each assembly and a locking washer to each screw.

To Dismantle the Points. Remove the flywheel as already described. Remove the spring clip and shim washer from the rocker arm pivot pin. Unscrew the nut and remove the locking washer from the rocker arm return spring assembly and gently ease the rocker arm and spring away. The fixed point is removed by unscrewing the lock-nut and then unscrewing the point. Should the points be pitted, gently ease their surfaces down

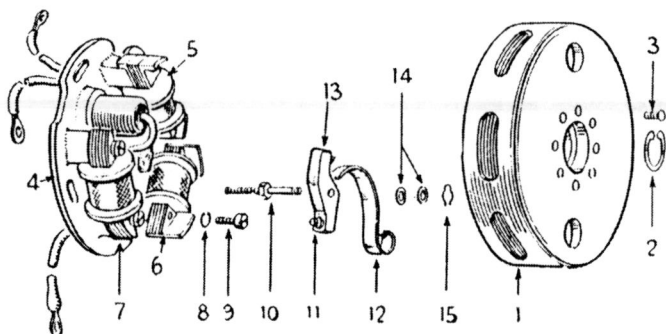

FIG. 28. FLYWHEEL MAGNETO

1. Flywheel assembly.	8. Spring washer.
2. Spring circlip (for extractor nut).	9. Coil securing screw.
3. Cam hub securing rivet.	10. Rocker arm pivot stud.
4. Backplate assembly.	11. Contact point.
5. Ignition coil.	12. Rocker arm return spring.
6. Lighting coil.	13. Contact-breaker rocker arm.
7. Lighting coil.	14. Shim washers.

15. Pivot stud spring clip.

with fine emery cloth; if badly pitted this suggests a faulty condenser.

Reassembly is in the reverse order, paying particular attention to the following—

1. A light film of Castrolease (heavy) grease on the pivot pin.
2. A smear of Castrolease (heavy) grease on the lubricating pad.
3. Fully tighten the flywheel fixing nut.
4. Adjust the points correctly.
5. If the backplate has been replaced to the scribed marks the ignition timing should be correct—$\frac{1}{4}$ in. before T.D.C. points open 0·001 in. Check that this is so using cigarette paper between the points.
6. Clean the sparking plug, and adjust the plug points (*see* page 77).

Spares and Renewals for General Maintenance (B.T.-H. Unit only). The following spares are given with the B.T.-H. ordering number and any spares or queries should be addressed to the makers—Messrs. British Thomson-Houston Co., Ltd., Coventry, England.

Description	Ordering Ref.
Alternator coil (R.H. side) . . .	SKC. 127572-G1
Alternator coil (L.H. side) . . .	SKC. 127572-G2
Ignition coil	SKC. 127573-G1
Adjustable contact (Fixed) . . .	SKC. 127410-G1
Backplate, Condenser, Contact-breaker Pivot and Lubricator pad assembly . . .	CZ. 127574-G1
Cam pad lubricator assembly . . .	SKC. 127453-G1
Condenser	CZ. 127476-G1
Earthing cable	SKC. 127466-G1
Rocker-arm assembly	SKC. 127421-G1
Retaining clip for rocker arm . . .	CR. 127418

CHAPTER XV

LIGHTS AND WIRING CIRCUIT

L.T. current for lighting and horn is supplied by two coils mounted on the flywheel assembly backplate. With few moving parts little maintenance is necessary. Check cables occasionally for loose connexions, particularly on the pick up terminal block, or possible chafing at the insulation. A short to earth from these causes will almost certainly render lights and horn inoperative and possibly may also cut out the ignition.

The various cables are covered with different coloured P.V.C. insulation for easy identification. These colours are listed below—

From the Flywheel Terminal Block

(1) Black from earth to switch.

(2) Yellow from L.T. terminal to resistor. (The resistor and Selenium rectifier are situated in the carburettor compartment. For easy access it is advisable to remove the fuel tank (*see* page 6).)

Battery Leads

(1) Negative to earth.

(1) Positive to rectifier. Black.

From Rectifier

(1) Brown to switch on handlebars.

(1) Black to battery positive.

From the Resistor

(1) Green to push-button on switch.

(1) Green to horn.

(1) Black to L.T. terminal of flywheel mag. (may be yellow).

Inside Handlebar Switch

(1) Green from resistor.

(1) Brown from rectifier.

(1) Black from earth on flywheel magneto.

(1) Yellow to full beam on headlamp main bulb.

(1) Dark blue to dipped beam on headlamp main bulb.

(1) Light blue to headlamp parking bulb.

(1) Red to tail light and speedometer bulb.

At Push Button on Handlebar Switch

(1) Purple on horn.

At Horn

(1) Purple from push-button on switch.
(1) Green from resistor.

At Headlamp

(1) Yellow from switch to full beam on main bulb.
(1) Dark blue from switch to dipped beam on main bulb.
(1) Light blue from switch to parking light bulb.

At Tail Lamp

(1) Red from switch.

At Speedometer

(1) Red from switch.

In the case of no lights from the battery when fitted (parking lights only) the battery connexions should be examined, after ascertaining that the bulbs are in working order.

The Battery. During charging, water is lost by gassing and by evaporation. This MUST be replaced to maintain the battery in a healthy condition.

Once every ten days, the battery lid should be removed, the vent plugs (3) unscrewed and the level of the electrolyte brought up to the top edge of the plates by adding DISTILLED WATER. NEVER smoke or use a naked light when examining the condition of the cells as there is a danger of fire from the gas coming off.

It is advisable to have the battery checked at least once every three months.

Specific gravity readings and their indications are as follows—

1·280 to 1·300	.	.	Cell fully charged
approx. 1·210	.	.	Cell approx. half discharged
Below 1·150	.	.	Cell fully discharged

The readings (taken with a small capacity hydrometer) should be approximately the same for each cell. If one cell gives a value very different from the other two, it may be that (*a*) electrolyte has been lost from this particular cell, or (*b*) there may be a short circuit between the plates and in this case the battery should be examined by the local Lucas Service Depot, or agent.

NEVER leave the battery in a discharged condition. If the machine is to be out of service for any length of time, the battery should be removed and fully charged, and at least once every two weeks given a refresher

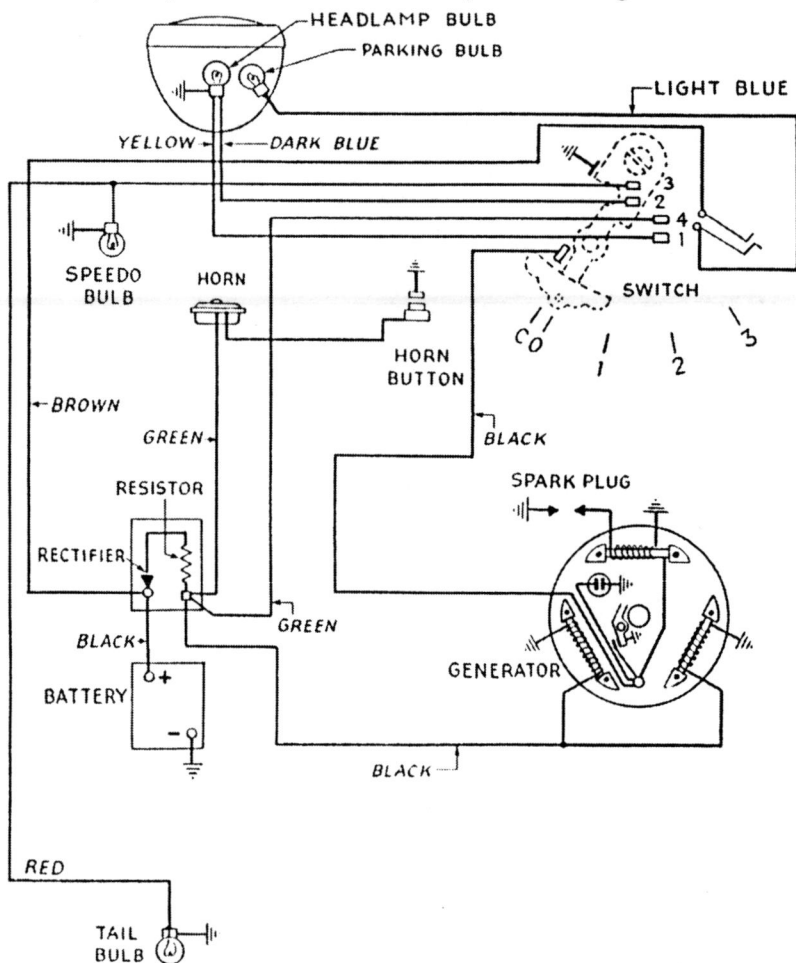

HEADLAMP BULB
PARKING BULB
LIGHT BLUE
YELLOW
DARK BLUE
SPEEDO BULB
HORN
SWITCH
HORN BUTTON
BROWN
GREEN
BLACK
RESISTOR
SPARK PLUG
RECTIFIER
BLACK
GREEN
BATTERY
GENERATOR
BLACK
RED
TAIL BULB

FIG. 29. LIGHTING AND WIRING CIRCUIT

charge to prevent the tendency for the plates to become permanently sulphated.

Electric Horn. Before leaving the makers, the horn is adjusted to give its best performance, and will give a very considerable amount of service without attention. There is no provision for subsequent adjustment as this is considered unnecessary. Should the horn not function correctly, check the following probable causes—

1. Horn loose in its mounting.
2. Wires to horn loose or adrift.
3. Wires to resistor loose or adrift.
4. Wire to horn button push loose or adrift.
5. Connexion between horn push and handlebar uncertain.

If all the above are in order, return the horn to the Vespa agent for replacement.

Testing of the lighting coils and rectifier requires special apparatus. Therefore, if the lights are in any way uncertain, it is strongly recommended that the machine be taken to the local Vespa or B.T.-H. agent for attention.

CHAPTER XVI

LUBRICATION INFORMATION

The following lubrication details are given as a guide to the correct grade of oils and greases to be used. It is most advisable to keep to one make and grade of oil for engine or gearbox. Failure to do this leads to rapid formation of carbon in the engine, gummed piston rings and subsequent formation of sludge-like deposit in the gear case.

ENGINE. Lubrication is by mixing oil with the petrol in the fuel tank. The correct proportions are (*see* filler cap for details)—

First 500 miles—Three-quarters of a pint of oil per gallon of petrol.

After 500 miles—Half a pint of oil per gallon of petrol.

Grade of oil, S.A.E. 30. (Typical example Castrol XL.)

GEAR BOX. Every 600 miles, drain the gearbox (*see* page 3) and refill to the correct level with similar S.A.E. 30 oil.

If Castrol XL is used in the gearbox, Castrol flushing oil can be used first, to remove all traces of the old oil.

FLYWHEEL MAGNETO GENERATOR (*see* page 60). There are two lubrication points only—

1. Felt pad to cam.
2. Fulcrum-pin of actuating point arm.

Lubricate by *grease* only, oil may find its way on to the points. Apply at intervals of 1,500 miles.

Grease—Castrolease (heavy).

FRONT SUSPENSION AND HUB (*see* page 22). Lubricate the front spindle of the oscillating arm at least once every 600 miles by means of a grease-gun (one grease nipple). Use one brand of grease for all greasing and grease gun operations.

FRONT HUB BEARINGS. Every 5,000 miles remove the dust cover (*see* maintenance chapter) and inject grease into the bearing cup.

REAR HYDRAULIC DAMPER (*see* page 29). If the damper is not functioning properly, it should be removed, drained, cleaned out and refilled (*see* page 31).

CONTROL LEVERS AND CABLES (*see* page 4). A few drops of light oil should be placed on the control lever pivot pins when maintenance is being carried out. In very cold conditions it may be found beneficial to use Castrol non-freeze cable lubricant or Bowden non-freeze cable grease.

The correct amount of one of the following upper cylinder lubricants, mixed with the petrol and oil mixture is to be thoroughly recommended:

Castrollo, Redex, Carburol.

During cold weather it is recommended that Redex be mixed with the oil in the gear box. The makers of Redex will supply details on application to Redex, 365, Chiswick High Road, London, W.1.

SPEEDOMETER GEARBOX. At least once every 1,000 miles the speedometer gearbox grease nipple should receive a single shot from the grease gun.

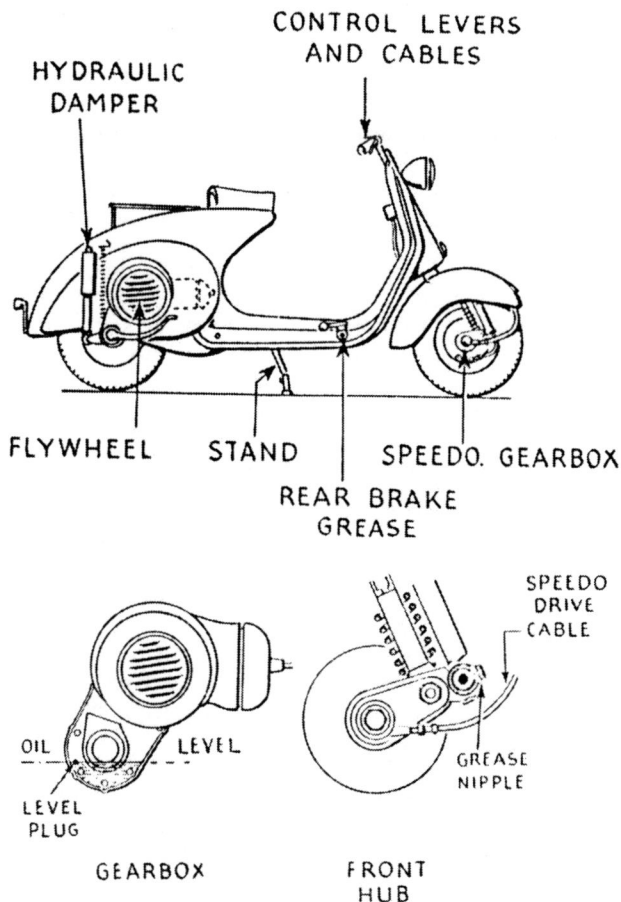

FIG. 30. LUBRICATION CHART

CHAPTER XVII

THE 42/L2 AND GRAN SPORT MODELS

A NUMBER of improvements and modifications have been introduced in the 42/L2 model, but in the main these do not involve any changes in dismantling and assembling procedure. The main points of difference between this model and its predecessors are enumerated below.

THE POWER UNIT. The new crankshaft incorporates a larger big-end bearing, designed to give longer life and to absorb the shocks naturally resulting from higher engine speeds.

FLYWHEEL MAGNETO. The only difference is that a gap of 0·015 in. has to be maintained between the contact points. The servicing and repair of the flywheel magneto is now undertaken solely by the service department, Douglas (Sales and Service), Ltd., Kingswood, Bristol.

EXHAUST SILENCER. A larger and improved exhaust silencer is now fitted, having the advantage of making for quieter running and diminishing the risk of "coking-up" in the engine. The method of fixing is the same, but unfortunately it is not possible to dismantle the silencer. However, overnight immersion in "Gunk Hydro-Seal" will assist in the removal of hard "coke" in inaccessible places.

IMPROVEMENTS. On this model the headlamp is mounted on the handlebar but wiring and colour charts remain the same. The speedometer is now incorporated in the headlamp, the operating cable passing through the steering column.

A hydraulic damper is incorporated in the front suspension, which is mounted upon cast and welded-on lugs on the steering column and the oscillating arm casting. The unit can be dismantled only by Douglas service agents since special tools are required.

Other improvements include a mud-and-water deflector on the rear brake, a larger battery, heavier control cables, increased fuel-tank capacity and an improved filler cap.

The spring for the new rear suspension arm is now built around the rear damper unit. This unit, like the front one, can be dismantled and serviced only by a Vespa agent.

TYRE PRESSURES ON THE 42/L2

	Pressure (lb per sq. in.)	
Solo—	Michelin	Pirelli
Front tyre . . .	17	14
Rear tyre . . .	23	14

With pillion passenger—

Front tyre	.	.	17	14
Rear tyre	.	.	30	32

An increase of 5 lb per sq. in. front and rear is recommended when a sidecar is fitted. (For the sidecar tyre pressure *see* Chapter IV.)

TECHNICAL INFORMATION

Capacity	.	.	.	. 123·67 c.c.
Bore	.	.	.	. 54 mm.
Stroke	.	.	.	. 54 mm.
Compression ratio		.	.	. 6·5: 1
Gear ratios (solo)	.	.	.	. 4·85: 1, 7·6: 1, 12·2: 1
Gear ratios (sidecar)	.	.	.	. 5·84: 1, 8·18: 1, 14·7: 1
Fuel tank capacity	.	.	.	. 1·37 imp. gallons
Tyre sizes	.	.	.	. 8 in. × 3·50 in.
Dry weight	.	.	.	. 190 lb.
Wheel base	.	.	.	. 46½ in.
Overall length	.	.	.	. 67½ in.
Overall height	.	.	.	. 40½ in.
Ground clearance	.	.	.	. 4 in.
Turning circle	.	.	.	. 59 in.

Gran Sport Model

The dismantling and assembling of the Gran Sport power unit is identical with that of the 42/L2 and its predecessors except in certain small details, which will be obvious to the owner.

POWER UNIT TECHNICAL INFORMATION

Horse-power	.	.	.	. 7·89 at 7,500 r.p.m.
Capacity	.	.	.	. 150 c.c.
Bore	.	.	.	. 57 mm.
Stroke	.	.	.	. 57 mm.
Compression ratio		.	.	. 7: 1.
Maximum speed	.	.	.	. 62 m.p.h.
Fuel consumption	.	.	.	. 93·2 m.p.g.
Gearbox	.	.	.	. 4-speed
Tyre sizes	.	.	.	. 10 in. × 3·50 in.

Brake drums have cast-on cooling fins.

Saddle	.	.	.	.	. Twin seat hinged at front
Weight dry	.	.	.	.	. 220·4 lb.

GEAR CHANGE MECHANISM IN THE 42/L2 AND GRAN SPORT MODELS. It will be noted that gear changing is effected by wire control cables as opposed to the rods and ball-jointed links used on other models.

To adjust the gear change cables proceed as follows—

Hold the end of the inner cable with a pair of pliers and after releasing the cable locking ferrule pull the cable until the twist grip is about to turn. Slide the locking ferrule up to its stop and tighten the bolt. Now select third gear, both on twist-grip and on gear shifter, and repeat the above operations for the other cable. Engage neutral gear. If correctly set there should be slight play. If not, pull back the rubber sleeve to reach the adjusting nut on the handlebars. Tension the cables by screwing back the adjusters.

If, when the cable tension is correct, the handlebar indications are wrong, this can be corrected by releasing one of the adjusters and tightening the other. Before removing any of the control cables from the chassis a length of thin copper wire should be secured to one end and pulled through with the old cable. By attaching the wire to the new cable and pulling the copper wire the new cable can easily be inserted.

APPENDIX A

FAULT-FINDING TABLE

ENGINE WILL NOT START. Make tests in following order—

Test 1. Are all controls set correctly? If not, position them as necessary—
Twist grip slightly open.
Carburettor flooded if engine quite cold.
If engine warm, the carburettor must *not* be flooded.
Carburettor choke closed if engine quite cold.
If engine warm, choke must be left open.

If O.K.

Test 2. Depress tickler to ascertain that carburettor will flood. If it does not—

Reason	Remedy
Petrol run out.	Set tap to reserve and refill with petrol and oil at next filling station.
Petrol tap closed.	Turn on.
Petrol pipe blocked.	Remove and clear.
Air vent in tank filler cap blocked.	Clear vent.

If O.K.

Test 3. Remove sparking plug and examine. If very wet and oily, trouble may be overrich mixture (*see* Test 4). If the plug is normally black and dry, lay it with the H.T. lead attached so that the body of the plug only touches the cylinder head. Work the kick-starter when the plug should spark regularly. If not—

Reason	Remedy
Defective plug.	Try another plug or dismantle this one and clean it, resetting gap on reassembly at 0·018 in. (*see* page 49).
C.B. arm sticking.	Clean and re-grease (*see* page 61).
C.B. points pitted.	Clean and face up (*see* page 62).
C.B. points out of adjustment.	Adjust (*see* page 61). B.T.-H. 0·012 in., Piaggio 0·016 in.

73

Reason	Remedy
Short in H.T. lead.	Renew lead (a most unlikely defect).
Short circuit in magneto.	Take to agents for check of insulation.
Handlebar cut-out switch stuck.	Examine and free off or take to agent.

Test 4. For overrich mixture—

Reason	Remedy
Tickler has been used excessively.	Turn off petrol, remove sparking plug. Turn engine over several times by kick-starter. Check that the plug sparks (Test 3). Replace plug. Start engine and turn on petrol after it fires.
Carburettor flooding.	Dismantle petrol pipe and float chamber (*see* page 32). Clean off all dirt and check that float is not punctured and that its needle seats correctly. Re-erect. Clear engine of excess fuel as in above test but turn on petrol before starting the engine.
Air filter choked.	Remove and clean (*see* page 32).
Choke plate sticking.	Free off and lubricate with light oil.
Carburettor setting incorrect.	Take to agents for resetting.

ENGINE WILL START BUT RUNS IMPERFECTLY

Test 5. A good engine should start within three kicks and continue to run evenly. If it does not, the cause will be either some act of negligence in maintenance or that the engine has been run overlong without attention.

Make a check by setting twist-grip partly open, petrol *not* turned on and handlebar cut-out switch in the *switched off* position. Press steadily on the kick-start pedal when good compression resistance should be felt. If not—

Reason	Remedy
Sparking plug may be loose.	Tighten and make sure washer is O.K.
Cylinder head joint loose.	Tighten head nuts.
Piston rings gummed in grooves.	Decarbonize.
Exhaust port choked.	Decarbonize.

If above O.K. erratic performance may fall in categories—

ENGINE STARTS BUT STOPS OF OWN ACCORD. Check further fuel faults to Test 2 as follows—

Carburettor.   Dismantle and check that air holes in float chamber cap are clear. Main jet is clear. Float not punctured. Induction pipe joint and joint of carburettor to induction pipe should both be tight, without leaks. Make sure main jet is screwed in tightly and needle valve of float chamber is seating.

Fuel.   Check that a good brand of petrol with correct proportion of oil is being used. Check there is no water in fuel (this can be seen as it will lie in globules on the floor of the tank or in the carburettor). If bad petrol or watered petrol has been obtained, it should be thrown away (taking full fire precautions).

Ignition.   There may be plug or magneto trouble as in Test 3.

ENGINE RUNS BUT WITH LACK OF POWER. If corrections by Test 5 have been made the following may be at fault—

Reason	Remedy
Silencer choked.	Dismantle and clean, especially baffle.
Brakes binding.	Readjust (*see* page 15).
Weak mixture.	If all foregoing tests O.K., consult agent as to revision of setting.
Condenser faulty.	Take to agent.

In case of any doubt refer to the section dealing with the suspect part.

APPENDIX B

TECHNICAL DATA

ENGINE DIMENSIONS AND PERFORMANCE

Bore	2·22 in. = 56·5 mm.
Stroke	1·97 in. = 49·8 mm.
Cubic capacity . . .	7·65 cu. in. = 124·858 c.c.
Compression ratio . . .	6·4: 1.
Max. performance . . .	4 b.h.p. at 4,500 r.p.m.

REBORING INSTRUCTIONS

Rebore to 0·020 in. when bore exceeds 0·008 in. on above figure.

GEAR RATIOS (Crankshaft to wheel 15 in. diameter)

1st gear . . .	12: 1
2nd gear . . .	7·5: 1
3rd gear . . .	4·78: 1

GENERAL MACHINE DIMENSIONS AND PERFORMANCE

Weight dry	approx. 170 lb.
Ground clearance . . .	5·9 in.
Overall height . . .	37½ in.
Overall length . . .	65 in.
Minimum turning circle . .	59 in. diameter.
Distance between wheel centres	44½ in.
Maximum climbing ability	1 in 5.

DESCRIPTION AND DIMENSIONS OF THE PRINCIPAL BUSHES AND BEARINGS

Description (numbers in brackets indicate quantity per machine where this exceeds one)	Dimensions (millimetres unless otherwise stated)		
	Dia.	Bore	Length or Width
Small-end bush	17 ×	15 ×	16
Crankshaft main ball race (2) . .	52 ×	20 ×	12
Crankshaft oil seal (2) . . .	36 ×	19 ×	9
Kick-starter gear ball race . . .	42 ×	20 ×	9
Layshaft main race (ball and roller) .	35 ×	15 ×	8
Final drive oil seal	42 ×	27 ×	10
Final drive shaft bearings			
Inner race L.20 N.	42 ×	20 ×	9
Outer race L.20 NB. . . .	42 ×	20 ×	9
Final drive tubular distance piece .	25 ×	21 ×	82
Front hub ball race R.H. . . .	40 ×	17 ×	12
Front hub ball race L.H. . . .	32 ×	12 ×	10

OTHER ENGINE DIMENSIONS

Piston ring (2) clearances—

> End gap . . . . 0·006 in.
> Vertical clearance . . . 0·003 in. to 0·005 in.

Crankshaft oil seal fitting flange (2) 49 × 1 mm.

OTHER GEARBOX AND CLUTCH DIMENSIONS

> Drive gear needle rollers (29) . . . 2·5 × 15·8 mm.
> Layshaft needle rollers (19) . . . 3 × 8 mm.
> Kick-starter actuating spring (2) free length . 17 mm ($\frac{11}{16}$) ins
> Clutch springs (6) free length . . . 1 in.

FINAL-DRIVE DETAILS

> Final drive axle nut split-pin . . . 1½ in. × ⅛ in.

BRAKES

> Brake lining (Ferodo recommended) (4) . . ⅛ × ¾ × 5 in.

LIGHTING, IGNITION AND PLUG DETAILS

> Contacts gap
> Piaggio mag. . . . 0·014 in. to 0·018 in.
> B.T.-H. mag. . . . 0·012 in.
> Spark plug gap . . . 0·018 in.
> Ignition timing . . . ¼ in. before T.D.C. points just opening

Headlamp bulb . . . 6 V 25/25 W double filament
Rear light bulb . . . 6 V 3 W SBC
Pilot light bulb . . . 6 V 3 W MBC
Speedometer bulb . . . 6 V 3 W MBC

CARBURETTOR DETAILS

Main jet 80
Needle jet . . . 105
Throttle valve . . . 3

CABLE LENGTHS

Inner speedometer cable . . . 39 in.
Clutch cable
Inner . . . . . . 70½ in.
Outer . . . . . 64¾ in.
Throttle cable
Inner . . . . . 69 3/32 in.
Outer . . . . . 64 11/32 in.
Front brake cable
Inner . . . . . 54⅛ in.
Outer . . . . . 46 1/16 in.
Rear brake cable
Inner . . . . . 34 in.
Outer . . . . 22¼ in.

APPENDIX C

DO'S AND DON'TS

"DO"

1. Have special regard to your petrol and oil mixture (*see* page 68).
2. Turn off the petrol when you stop to avoid possible flooding.
3. Run the machine when finally stopping for the day with the petrol and oil mixture switched off, to drain the carburettor.
4. After standing for any length of time sway the machine from side to side to mix the petrol and oil *before* pulling the fuel tap to "on."
5. Operate the kick-starter once or twice with the clutch lever raised to free possible dragging of the clutch plates (especially during cold weather).
6. Occasionally open and close the throttle when using the engine as a brake when descending long hills as in the closed position the engine receives no lubrication.
8. Check regularly the gearbox oil level.
9. Check tyres weekly and maintain at the correct pressure (*see* page 11).
10. Switch on the lights, in all positions, once a week to ensure correct operation should the occasion of night riding arise.
11. Carry a spare clean plug of the correct grade.

"DON'T"

1. Twist the gear change mechanism when the engine is at rest.
2. Use choke control when the engine is warm.
3. Abuse your machine.
4. Let the engine slog, change to a lower gear.
5. Slip the clutch, its use is only for starting and stopping.
6. Leave your brakes to the last few yards in icy or wet weather, test them occasionally.
7. Lean the machine to the off side with the petrol tap in the "on" position in case petrol mixture drains into the crankcase.
8. Go haphazardly about maintenance or repairs. Follow a routine.
9. And finally, DON'T put off till tomorrow what should be done today.

INDEX

OTHER CLASSIC MOTORCYCLE MANUALS CURRENTLY AVAILABLE IN THIS SERIES:

ARIEL WORKSHOP MANUAL 1933-1951

A comprehensive manual for all models built between 1933 and 1951. *Four cylinder:* 4/F/600cc OHC, 4/F/600cc OHV, 4/G/1,000cc OHV (Cast Iron & Light Alloy). *Twin cylinder:* 500cc OHV models KG & KH. *Single cylinder:* 600cc SV model VB. 500cc OHV models VG & VH. 350cc OHV models NH & NG. 250cc OHV models OH, OG, LG & LH. Much of the data is applicable to later models that utilize these same engines.

ISBN: 1-58850-071-3

BMW FACTORY WORKSHOP MANUAL R50, R50S, R60, R69S

A reproduction of the factory workshop manual for the R50, R50S, R60, R69S twin cylinder series of BMW's. Also included is a supplement for the USA models: R50US, R60US, R69US.

The text and illustration captions are printed in English, German, French and Spanish and while the translations may at times be a little quirky, the data is comprehensive and invaluable to the BMW enthusiast.

ISBN: 1-58850-067-5

BMW FACTORY WORKSHOP MANUAL R27, R28

A reproduction of the factory workshop manual for the R27 and R28 single cylinder series of BMW's, while quite scarce in the USA these were very popular models in Europe.

The text and illustration captions are printed in English, German, French and Spanish and while the translations may at times be a little quirky, the data is comprehensive and invaluable to the BMW enthusiast.

ISBN: 1-58850-068-3

DUCATI OHC FACTORY WORKSHOP MANUAL

This fully illustrated Factory manual covers the 160cc, 250cc and 350cc narrow case, Single Cylinder, OHC series of Ducati motorcycles including the 160 Monza Junior, 250 Monza, 250GT, 250 Mark 3, 250 Mach1, 250 Motocross and the 350 Sebring. As expected from a factory publication this manual includes complete technical data and comprehensive detailed instructions for the repair and overhaul of all major and minor mechanical and electrical components, making it an invaluable resource for collectors and restorers of these classic Ducati motorcycles.

ISBN: 978-1-58850-103-5

HONDA FACTORY WORKSHOP MANUAL

A faithful reproduction of the 1967 Floyd Clymer publication of the official Honda Factory Workshop Manual for the 250-300 series C72, C77, CS72, CS77, CB72, CB77 (Hawk).

There are exhaustive tables of technical data, tolerances and fits and all of the expected data from a factory publication for the repair and overhaul of all major and minor mechanical and electrical components, making it an invaluable resource for collectors and restorers of these classic Honda motorcycles.

There are 245 illustrations and each procedure is explained in a step-by-step method using an appropriate illustration. The translation from Japanese to English is, at times, a little quirky but the profuse illustrations make up for any difficulty in understanding what needs to be done!

ISBN: 1-58850-073-X

HONDA MAINTENANCE & REPAIR MANUAL 1960-1966

A faithful reproduction of the John Thorpe BOOK OF THE HONDA a fully illustrated repair and maintenance manual that covers the 50cc models C100, C102, Monkey Bike, CE105H Trails Bike, C110 & C114. The 125cc models C92, CB92 & Benley. The 250cc models C72 & CB72. The 305cc models C77, CB77. Originally published in 1967 by Floyd Clymer this illustrated manual contains repair and maintenance data for both Kick and Electric Start models including Electrical and Ignition Equipment, Wiring Diagrams, Clutch, Carburetion, Transmission, Forks, Engine, Brakes and more. It also includes information on routine service, maintenance and tune ups plus technical specification charts. While not as exhaustive as a factory manual there is adequate detailed text and diagrams to assist in major refurbishing such as an engine rebuild or even a complete mechanical renovation.

ISBN: 978-1-58850-102-8

NORTON FACTORY TWIN CYLINDER WORKSHOP MANUAL 1957-1970

A reproduction of the factory workshop manual for both the *Lightweight Twins:* 250cc Jubilee, 350cc Navigator and 400cc Electra and the *Heavyweight Twins:* Model 77, 88, 88SS, 99, 99SS, Sports Special, Manxman, Mercury, Atlas, G15, P11, N15, Ranger (P11A) which makes this manual appropriate for all Norton models that utilized this series of 500, 600, 650 and 750cc engines through the 1970 model year.

ISBN: 1-58850-069-1

NORTON MAINTENANCE & REPAIR MANUAL 1932-1939

All Pre-War SV, OHV and OHC models: 16H, 16I, 18, 19, 20, 50, 55, ES2, CJ, CSI, International models 30 & 40. Much of the data is applicable to both earlier and later models that utilize the following single cylinder engines: 490cc SV, 633cc SV, 348cc OHV, 490cc OHV, 596cc OHV, 348cc OHC, 490cc OHC. **ISBN: 1-58850-070-5**

TRIUMPH 1935-1939 MAINTENANCE & REPAIR MANUAL

All Pre-War single & twin cylinder models: L2/1, 2/1, 2/5, 3/1, 3/2, 3/5, 5/1, 5/2, 5/3, 5/4, 5/5, 5/10, 6/1, Tiger 70, Tiger 80, Tiger 90, 2H, Tiger 70C, 3S, 3H, Tiger 80C, 5H, Tiger 90C, 6S, 2HC, 3SC, 5T Speed Twin, 5S and T100 Tiger 100.

Much of the data is applicable to earlier models that utilize the following engines: *Single Cylinder:* 250cc OHV, 350cc SV, 350cc OHV, 500cc SV, 500cc OHV, 550cc SV and 600cc SV. *Twin Cylinder:* 500cc OHV and 650cc OHV. **ISBN: 1-58850-066-7**

TRIUMPH 1937-1951 WORKSHOP MANUAL (A. St. J. Masters)

The most comprehensive Workshop Manual available for pre swing-arm Triumph motorcycles. Covers rigid frame and sprung hub single cylinder SV & OHV and twin cylinder OHV pre-war, military, and post-war models: 2H, Tiger 70, Tiger 70C, 3S, 3H, Tiger 80, Tiger 80C, 5H, Tiger 90, Tiger 90C, 6S, 2HC, 3SC, 5T Speed Twin, 5S, T100 Tiger 100, 3HW, 3SW, 5SW, 3T, Grand Prix, TR5 Trophy and 6T Thunderbird.

Much of the data is applicable to earlier models that utilize the following engines: *Single Cylinder*: 250cc OHV, 350cc SV, 350cc OHV, 500cc SV, 500cc OHV and 600cc SV. *Twin Cylinder:* 350cc OHV, 500cc OHV and 650cc OHV. **ISBN: 1-58850-064-0**

TRIUMPH 1945-1955 FACTORY WORKSHOP MANUAL NO.11

The most comprehensive Workshop Manual available for pre-unit, twin-cylinder Triumph motorcycles. Covers the full line of rigid frame, sprung hub, swing-arm and 350cc models: 5T Speed Twin, T100 Tiger 100, TR5 Trophy, 6T Thunderbird, T110 Tiger 110 and 3T De-Luxe.

Much of the data is applicable to later models that utilize the following engines: Twin Cylinder 350cc OHV, 500cc OHV and 650cc OHV. **ISBN: 1-58850-065-9**

VESPA SERVICE & REPAIR MANUAL 1951-1961

Covers all 125cc and 150cc widemount engined Vespas from 1951 through 1961 beginning with the Vespa 125 (VM1T) through the GS150 (VS51T). It also covers the Douglas 42L2 and Clubman. This book includes all of the necessary information required for general maintenance and service of the widemount series of Vespa Scooters and there is adequate detailed text and diagrams to assist in major refurbishing such as an engine rebuild or even a complete mechanical renovation. **ISBN: 978-1-58850-113-4**

VINCENT WORKSHOP MANUAL 1935-1955

Complete technical data, service and maintenance information, and comprehensive detailed instructions for the repair and overhaul of all major and minor mechanical and electrical components for all models of Vincent motorcycles from 1935 through 1955. Also includes a detailed electrical section and a comprehensive chapter on modifications for racing.
ISBN: 1-58850-072-1

PLEASE CHECK OUR WEBSITE OR CONTACT YOUR DEALER FOR AVAILABILITY
~ WWW.VELOCEPRESS.COM ~

OTHER CLASSIC MOTORCYCLE MANUALS COMING SOON IN THIS SAME SERIES:

ARIEL MAINTENANCE & REPAIR MANUAL 1932-1939
LF3, LF4, LG, NF3, NF4, NG, OG, VA, VA3, VA4, VB, VF3, VF4, VG, Red Hunter LH, NH, OH, VH & Square Four 4F, 4G, 4H. This particular manual has a very good section dealing with the 1933 to 1936 four cylinder OHC engine and required reading if you own one of these rare motorcycles.

BRIDGESTONE FACTORY WORKSHOP MANUAL
50 Sport, 60 Sport, 90 De Luxe, 90 Trail, 90 Mountain, 90 Sport, 175 Dual Twin & Hurricane

HONDA FACTORY WORKSHOP MANUAL
125 & 150cc C.92, CS.92, CB.92, C.95 & CA.95

HONDA FACTORY WORKSHOP MANUAL
50cc ~ 100, 110, C.100 & C.110

INDIAN PARTS CATALOG ~ 50cc MINI BIKES
A fully illustrated parts manual for the 69 series mini bikes, absolutely essential information for anyone that owns, maintains, repairs, or is in the process of restoring a Ponybike, Boy Racer or Papoose.

SUZUKI FACTORY WORKSHOP MANUAL 250/200cc
T10, T20 [X-6 Hustler] T200 [X-5 Invader & Sting Ray]

VILLIERS ENGINE WORKSHOP MANUAL
All Villiers engines and ancillaries through 1947

BRITISH MILITARY MAINTENANCE & REPAIR MANUAL
Service & Repair data for all British WD motorcycles

BRITISH MOTORCYCLE ENGINES
AJS, Ariel, BSA, Excelsior, JAP, Norton, Royal Enfield, Rudge, Scott, Sunbeam, Triumph, Velocette, Villiers & Vincent ~ a compilation of 1950's articles from *The Motor Cycle* dealing with engine design.

PLEASE CHECK OUR WEBSITE OR CONTACT YOUR DEALER FOR AVAILABILITY
~ WWW.VELOCEPRESS.COM ~

9 781588 501134